Scrapbook

LIARS and LAWYERS

The Truth Behind Arkansas's Yankee Garbage Invasion

And The Politics To Stop It

By: D Gray Varnadore

This book is dedicated

To

Joseph Cody Varnadore

1986 – 2011

This book is dedicated to Joseph Cody Varnadore, my son who is no longer with us on this earth. However, Cody had a plan, and a portion of the profits from this book will go to The Varnadore Foundation, which will fund, but not limited to, Juvenile Leukemia Cancer Research at the Arkansas Children's Hospital in Little Rock, Arkansas, Scholarships for the Oil and Gas program at the University of Arkansas at Morrilton, and Environmental Preservation.

Cody touched a lot of people in his short life on earth and will continue to shine through his foundation. Cody had a caring heart and wanted to help others that were less fortunate.

Acknowledgments

I would like to thank the following people for their story's, photos and cartoons. As well as those that helped me organize all the documentation and edit the story.

First to the writers of all the news articles, not that I agree with all the stories, but this book would not be what it is without the news stories. Like Gazette's Scotts Van Laningham and Carline Decker and Ernest Dumas. The Democrat Don Johnson and Larry Ault. Democrat-Gazette, Rachel O'Neal, Jake Sandlin Andy Gotlieb and Joe Farmer. Stuttgart Daily Leader Keith Talley. Arkansas Times, Richard Martin and Pine Bluff Commercial, Elizabeth Wright. The photographer, Democrat-Gazette, Scott Carpenter and Cartoonist, Vic Harville, Deering and Scallion. To Ebenezer Bowles for compiling all the information. Also Sarah Woolf, for copies, e-mails and organizational help. JoAnn Snapp for editing. And to my wife Amy, who love and strength has helped us to endure the toughest of times. And is still the light of my life.

LIARS and LAWYERS

The Truth Behind the Yankee Garbage Invasion

By

D. Gray Varnadore

Recently I was going through a closet looking for an old note book when the top of a box fell to the floor. While picking the top up off the floor, I noticed the newspaper article that glared at me reminding me of a time when our on government conspired to put my company out of business.

It still ticks me off, some twenty plus years later, to know I lost the farm because of then Governor Bill Clinton's legislation that gave Waste Management a monopoly while forcing out all landfill competition, my business being one of the targets.

Instead of just putting the top back on the box, I decided to give it one more look. Then I decided, I'll make it into a scrap book and I'll be the narrator. Liars and Lawyers: The Truth behind the Yankee Garbage Invasion.

My scrapbook is a look back at the news articles, legal documents, legislation, and letters from regulators, Arkansas Department of Pollution Control &Ecology (ADPC&E), and then Governor Bill Clinton.

From Bankruptcy Court, to Eighth Circuit Court decisions, to all the liars and lawyers that were involved, this book will give you a firsthand look into how the State of Arkansas illegally regulated me right out of business.

*****

Back Ground

I grew up in the small, southern town of DeWitt, Arkansas. DeWitt is in the southeast part of Arkansas where rice and soy bean farming was and still is the main industry. The area is a place where farms are passed from one generation to the next and property doesn't change hands very often.

Our farm had seen a couple of generations before I was born. My dad, John Carl Varnadore, a World War II veteran, came back from the war and started a construction company. For over fifty years John Carl (as he was known) cleared land, built roads, and hunted ducks.

During his working years my dad cleared right-of-ways for AP&L from one side of the state to the other. I remember him talking about the different terrain and the challenges he encountered while clearing the right-of-way between Ft. Smith and West Memphis.

But my dad was a dirt man and knew dirt, so it was no surprise in 1976 when the Arkansas County Judge Bobby Ashcraft came to John Carl and asked him if he might consider putting in a landfill. Seems the City of Dewitt and the County were cited for running an open and burning dump by EPA and were looking for somebody else to handle the garbage issue.

My dad had just the location for a landfill. There was an eighty acre parcel of land on the south end of the farm where we had been running cattle and deer hunting. It was not in cultivation and had good clay content. The parcel was about eight miles from the City of DeWitt. There were only three homes within a mile of the property and the area was serviced by a county road.

*****

Permitting the Landfill

The permitting process for a Class 1 Landfill in 1979 was a three year process. From public notice, to public hearing, to actually receiving the permit took about three years. It was always hurry up and wait for the next hurdle to come along. And believe me there were a lot of hurdles to deal with in permitting a landfill.

In March of 1982 Varnadore Sanitary Landfill received a permit to dispose of Class 1 waste or household waste as we know it. The permit also allowed the disposal of non-hazardous, special waste like ash, sludge and baled municipal solid wastes.

Arkansas County was the only steady customer we had coming to the landfill. John Carl and the Mayor of DeWitt, Johnny Schallhorn, got into a stalemate over a fifty cents rate increase, so the City of DeWitt went to Stuttgart, twenty-five miles away one way. As a result, our new, empty landfill rocked along for the first five years receiving less than fifty tons of waste a day.

In May 1986 the ADPC&E had issued the Landfill and Administrative Consent Order to have groundwater monitoring wells installed and have a geotechnical and hydrogeological study performed to determine the site suitability. This is where I came on the scene. I had been employed Brown-Ferris Industries from 1984 -1986 when I moved home to help with the family business.

Mark Witherspoon was Chief of Solid Waste at ADPC&E at the time and contacted me about hiring a qualified engineering firm to conduct the study. The Grubbs, Garner and Hoskyn Firm was hired to conduct the study. The study concluded that our site was a diamond in the rough as far as landfill geology is concerned. The study determined that there was 60+ feet of clay with impermeability factors ranging from $K=1.2 \times 10(-8)$ with the first aquifer at 90 feet. According to every engineering firm that reviewed our study this landfill was one of the highest quality facilities in the South.

*****

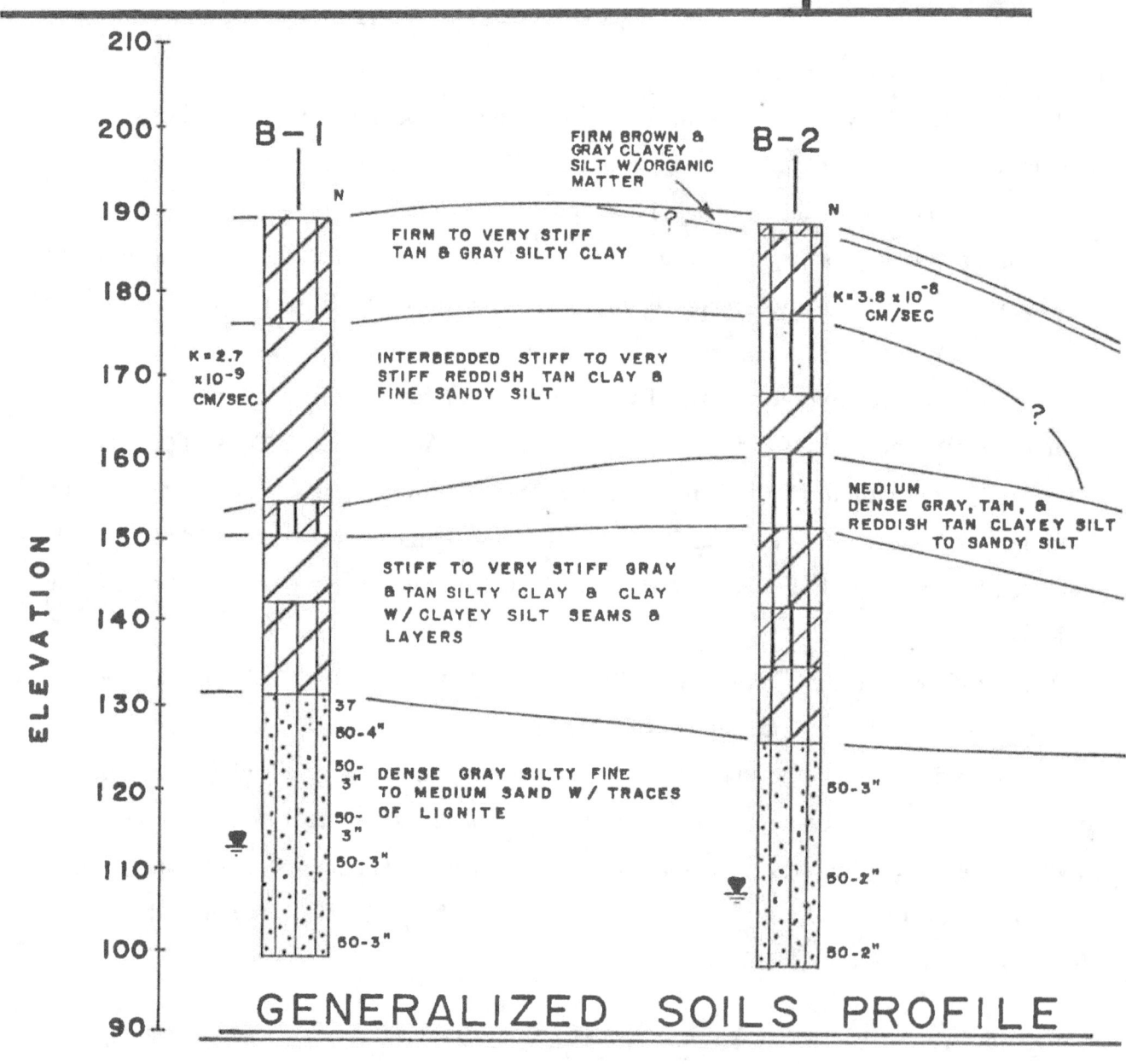

GENERALIZED SOILS PROFILE

VARNADORE LANDFILL

4

Beginning of Success Turned to Failure

On a June afternoon in 1987, I was in town at mother and daddy's house talking to him about the landfill. A white car pulled into the drive way. I was sitting on the sink and turned around to see the red State ADPC&E sticker on the car door.

"What are they doing coming here to the house? That's odd." I said.

Out of the car popped two dark headed men. I could tell they were from off but were with a state ADPC&E employee, Ken Beard. They knocked on the door, entered, and introduced themselves. They were from Redding, Pennsylvania and they were interested in sending us garbage from Philadelphia. They wanted to fly us back east to see their operation. Ken said the state knew we needed the volume, and there was a landfill capacity shortage in the north east. Within a week we were on our way to Philly.

The trip to Pennsylvania was to see the way they handle garbage in the northeast. Large volumes of garbage were dumped at transfer stations and processed. The sheer volume of waste they were handling on a daily basis at the transfer station was outrageous.

They handled the volume of two thousand tons per day with precision. The waste was separated, half in loose baled, open top, walking floor trailers and the other half was baled and loaded into van trailers or rail cars, then shipped to landfills throughout the Midwest. The number of carting (garbage) companies in Philly alone was amazing. Everywhere you looked there was a garbage truck and by a different company name.

After we got a quick tour of their facility they took us to play golf and I kept noticing this white pipe running down the side of the course. Well, after the third hole I had to ask.

"What's all the piping?" I asked.

"We're playing on a closed landfill, and they are using the gas from the landfill to make power," our Redding hosts told me.

"What a good idea!" I said and we played on. I thought why couldn't we do something like that and set up for gas production on our new landfill?

So that's what I did. When we got back from Philly, I got on the phone to our engineer to get started on a major permit modification to handle high volumes of waste. This was a long process between engineers drafting plans and ADPC&E reviewing plans, I began to wonder if we were ever going to get a revised permit.

I contacted some of my Brown Ferris Waste buddies, a company I used to work for, and they turned me on to O'Brien Energy System, Inc. O'Brien was the industry leader in managing of landfill gas and turning it into energy.

I called and talked to a young lady that answered the phone. I told her what my plan was and that I needed to talk to someone that could help me. She sent me to Douglas C. Nielsen. He just happened to be the Eastern Regional Manager of Bio-Gas Division.

Mr. Nielsen was excited about the opportunity help design a project to facilitate high volumes of waste that in turn could generate high volumes of gas to power generators to make electricity.   .

Even though we were looking at different companies and waste streams than the one we started out with, we kept ADPC&E fully in the loop and informed.

The state news media picked up on the landfill crises in the northeast US and the interest in Arkansas as a potential dumping ground. They also knew my dad had the landfill in question concerning northeast waste.

The article printed in the Arkansas Gazette on May 16, 1988, was the first I remember printed about northeast garbage. The media were trying to drag Harold Ives into being the one transporting the waste back to Arkansas.

I had talked to Harold about shipping waste from the northeast; we talked about using dedicated containers for the materials in question, but no deal was ever agreed upon. The stories escalated with rumors that had no fact or truth nevertheless, the media had Ives Trucking hauling northeast garbage to Arkansas in the same containers he was carrying Nabisco cookies.

Needless to say Harold Ives Trucking never hauled or had anything to do with importing garbage to Arkansas or anywhere else for that matter, nevertheless, the news media was looking for a smelly story.

The media and the public were so obsessed with the possibility of garbage being imported from New York, City, "Yankee Garbage", and that the state was going to become a dumping ground, the public was frantic. Continued on pg. **12.**

Northeast looking at Arkansas to dump its garbage

By Scott Van Laningham
GAZETTE STAFF

A private landfill near DeWitt recently was considered for disposal of garbage generated in the northeastern United States, and that may be a portent of things to come.

"At the present time, the deal is off," John Varnadore, owner of the Varnadore landfill about five miles east of DeWitt, said in a telephone interview late last week.

But he added, "If somebody comes up with a nice big contract, I wouldn't have any objections" to resurrecting the plan.

A state official acknowledged that hauling garbage to Arkansas from the Northeast — where land for landfills is at a premium — could happen in the future.

The cost of land for a new landfill in the Northeast means that the dumping prices can run up to $70 or $80 a ton, compared with $7 or $8 a ton at an Arkansas landfill, according to state Pollution Control and Ecology Department figures.

Varnadore declined to identify the potential source of the trash. He also declined to discuss details of the plan, but that it called for the garbage from the Northeast to be buried in the landfill he owns in Arkansas County.

Officials who asked not to be identified said the residential and commercial trash, none of it toxic waste, apparently would have come from Pennsylvania and New Jersey.

The plan reportedly called for about 500 tons of garbage a day eventually to be hauled to the landfill. That's about 150 tons a day more garbage than is generated by Little Rock and the rest of Pulaski County south of the Arkansas River.

Paul Means, state Pollution Control and Ecology Department director, said late last week that Varnadore had talked to Department officials, but no official application had been filed.

If the proposal resurfaces, Varnadore would have to revise engineering plans for the landfill, and that would require a public hearing, Means said.

Means said the idea of garbage being brought to Arkansas from other states made him nervous, but the state can't prohibit it.

Federal courts have ruled that hauling garbage from one state to another state for disposal constitutes interstate commerce that could be prohibited only for "appropriate environmental reasons," Means said.

Varnadore has a state permit to operate an 80-acre landfill, with the potential to expand to an adjacent 120 acres. DeWitt and Arkansas County now dump trash at the landfill.

Arkansas County Judge Bobby Ashcraft said he has heard "rumors" for several months about the plan to bring in out-of-state garbage, but nothing official has been presented to him or the Quorum Court.

Ashcraft said Varnadore had said that only ash from incinerated garbage, not the garbage itself, would have been hauled to the landfill.

Another official said the plan called for residential and commercial garbage, as well as ash.

Means said that if ash from a trash incinerator were dumped at the landfill, the ash would have to be tested to determine what is in it.

Ashcraft said he also had discussed with Harold Ives, owner of Harold Ives Trucking Company at Stuttgart, the possibility of Ives' trucks hauling the ash to Varnadore's landfill. Ashcraft said Ives was looking for something to haul back to Arkansas from the Northeast so his trucks would not have to make the return trip empty.

Alan Johnston, president of Ives Trucking, confirmed that Ives "was approached about transporting household waste" to Varnadore's landfill.

"I have serious business and personal concerns and I don't believe it would be in the best interest of Arkansas or Harold Ives Trucking," Johnston said.

Johnston said he did not know whose idea it was. Johnston said, "The more [Ives] found out about it, the less he liked it." After looking into the plan, "we've rejected any participation" by the trucking firm, he said.

Ives was appointed to the state Game and Fish Commission last year by Governor Bill Clinton. The Varnadore landfill is about eight miles west of the White River Wildlife Refuge and is visible from state Highway 153, a major access to the wildlife refuge.

The Pollution Control and Ecology Department cited Varnadore's landfill in December 1986 for "chronic violations" of state landfill regulations. The landfill was cited for not submitting groundwater analysis for a year and half, not placing adequate ground cover over filled sections and improper handling of some materials, such as dead animals and tires. Varnadore agreed to pay a $150 fine and correct the problems. He has not been cited for further violations.

Rumors Floating In DeWitt; John Varnadore Says No To Negotiating

Rumors are floating around DeWitt again about Varnadore's Landfill being used as a dumping place for waste and garbage from areas across the United States.

Mark Whitherspoon with the Pollution Control and Ecology Department said that John Carl Varnadore, owner of Varnadore Landfill, located east of DeWitt, had not turned in a request to modify his permit (which is necessary if he plans to dump out of state waste at his landfill) but if and when he does make such a request a public hearing will have to be held and it will be held in DeWitt.

Mayor John Schallhorn said that he talked with Lt. Governor Winston Bryant and that as of Tuesday no permit or additional permit had been requested. Mayor Schallhorn said that Lt. Gov. Bryant suggested that a formal group be formed and a spokesperson for the group be appointed and that other groups, such as Ducks Unlimited, Arkansas Wildlife Federation, other clubs, PC&E and the Governor's office should be advised how they feel about the proposed increase in dumping.

(The Governor's office was contacted today (Tuesday) by the Era-Enterprise about phone calls made to the Governor opposing the proposal. Mike Gaulding of the Governor's office said some calls had been made about the proposal but the office does not keep a count on phone calls.)

The mayor said that there has been a comment made that "what is not non-toxic, non hazardous and non infectious today may not be so tomorrow." He said, "The combination of chemicals

(Continued on page 8)

that a letter of intent to haul from Pine Bluff to Varnadore Landfill had been revoked with another letter stating he would not haul waste and garbage.

The letters were to Interstate Waste and Disposal, Inc. of Little Rock.

Mr. Varnadore made this statement to the Era-Enterprise "I am not negotiating with anyone at this time to dump out of state garbage and waste in Varnadore Landfill."

Arkansas County Judge Bobby Ashcraft said the Arkansas County Quorum Court had no say so over the private landfill and had not voted on the dumping proposal for out of state garbage and waste at the landfill. It was rumored that the Quorum Court had voted to support the proposal.

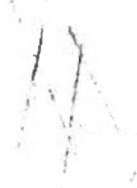

O'BRIEN ENERGY SYSTEMS

January 13, 1989

The Powerhouse
Since 1915

Listed on:
American Stock Exchange
Philadelphia Stock Exchange
Symbol: OBS

Mr. Gray Varnadore
Arkansas County Waste
P. O. Box 387
DeWitt, AR 72042

Dear Mr. Varnadore:

I am enclosing information about O'Brien Energy's landfill gas recovery capabilities. We presently have 5 gas to energy plants in operation, three under construction, and several more in the final stages of development. We are very interested in the concept of recovering gas from your balefill since we have already spent a good amount of time in developing that same concept for a project at a Caribbean nation.

I have also initiated steps to see if our shipping associates would be interested in providing prices to deliver baled wastes from the North Eastern United States to the mouth of the Mississippi and then up the Mississippi to mile marker 557. When I get their response on this, I will notify you. However, rather than simply quoting you a price for handling the refuse, we are interested in hauling our own baled waste from the North East to your site. Can you supply me with the price ($/yd^3) you would charge for baled waste delivered to your gate. Assume that you would receive 50,000 ton shipments every two weeks.

Very truly yours,

Douglas C. Nielsen
Eastern Regional Manager
BioGas Division

DCN:jm

Enc.

Philadelphia Office:
225 South Eighth Street
Philadelphia, PA 19106

Phone: 215-627-5500
FAX: 215-923-5227

National Historic Register
1987

POWER GENERATION -30

LFG ANALYSIS FOR DEWITT1 LANDFILL
Assumed Decompostion Rate is <u>AVERAGE</u>   Trash in Place = 12600.00 Tons

YEAR	TRASH (1) TONS/YR	CH4 (2) MSCFD	KW/HR(3)	$$ELEC (4) (000)	$$GAS (5) (000)
1991	600.00	0.00			
1992	600.00	0.00			
1993	600.00	304.80			
1994	600.00	609.60	1743.5	697.4	667.5
1995	600.00	794.40	2272.0	908.8	869.9
1996	600.00	979.20	2800.5	1120.2	1072.2
1997	600.00	1164.00	3329.0	1331.6	1274.6
1998	600.00	1348.80	3857.6	1543.0	1476.9
1999	600.00	1533.60	4386.1	1754.4	1679.3
2000	600.00	1718.40	4914.6	1965.8	1881.6
2001	600.00	1903.20	5443.2	2177.3	2084.0
2002	600.00	2088.00	5971.7	2388.7	2286.4
2003	600.00	2272.80	6500.2	2600.1	2488.7
2004	600.00	2457.60	7028.7	2811.5	2691.1
2005	600.00	2642.40	7557.3	3022.9	2893.4
2006	600.00	2827.20	8085.8	3234.3	3095.8
2007	600.00	3012.00	8614.3	3445.7	3298.1
2008	600.00	3196.80	9142.8	3657.1	3500.5
2009	600.00	3381.60	9671.4	3868.6	3702.9
2010	600.00	3566.40	10199.9	4080.0	3905.2
2011	600.00	3751.20	10728.4	4291.4	4107.6
2012	0.00	3769.20	10779.9	4312.0	4127.3
2013	0.00	3870.60	11069.9	4428.0	4238.3
2014	0.00	3667.20	10488.2	4195.3	4015.6
2015	0.00	3463.80	9906.5	3962.6	3792.9
2016	0.00	3380.40	9667.9	3867.2	3701.5
2017	0.00	3297.00	9429.4	3771.8	3610.2
2018	0.00	3213.60	9190.9	3676.4	3518.9
2019	0.00	3130.20	8952.4	3580.9	3427.6
2020	0.00	3046.80	8713.8	3485.5	3336.2
2021	0.00	2963.40	8475.3	3390.1	3244.9
2022	0.00	2880.00	8236.8	3294.7	3153.6
2023	0.00	2796.60	7998.3	3199.3	3062.3
2024	0.00	2713.20	7759.8	3103.9	2971.0

THE NET PRESENT VALUE OF THE $$ GAS @ 12.5% DISCOUNT RATE IS 17248.4

NOTES:
(1) Recorded annual placement of trash in 1000 tons.
(2) Methane generated each year in 1000 SCF per day.
(3) KW available based on (2) at a rate of 350 CFD/1000 KW
(4) Electric revenue based on (3) at $.05/kwhr,8000 hrs/yr
(5) Annual value of gas (2) at a rate of $3.00/mmBTU

10

LFG ANALYSIS FOR DEWITT1 LANDFILL   Trash in Place = 12600.00 Tons
   Assumed Decompostion Rate is AVERAGE

YEAR	TRASH (1) TONS/YR	CH4 (2) MSCFD	KW/HR(3)	$$ELEC (4) (000)	$$GAS (5) (000)
1991	600.00	0.00			
1992	600.00	0.00			
1993	600.00	304.80	1743.5	697.4	667.5
1994	600.00	609.60	2272.0	908.8	869.9
1995	600.00	794.40	2800.5	1120.2	1072.2
1996	600.00	979.20	3329.0	1331.6	1274.6
1997	600.00	1164.00	3857.6	1543.0	1476.9
1998	600.00	1348.80	4386.1	1754.4	1679.3
1999	600.00	1533.60	4914.6	1965.8	1881.6
2000	600.00	1718.40	5443.2	2177.3	2084.0
2001	600.00	1903.20	5971.7	2388.7	2286.4
2002	600.00	2088.00	6500.2	2600.1	2488.7
2003	600.00	2272.80	7028.7	2811.5	2691.1
2004	600.00	2457.60	7557.3	3022.9	2893.4
2005	600.00	2642.40	8085.8	3234.3	3095.8
2006	600.00	2827.20	8614.3	3445.7	3298.1
2007	600.00	3012.00	9142.8	3657.1	3500.5
2008	600.00	3196.80	9671.4	3868.6	3702.9
2009	600.00	3381.60	10199.9	4080.0	3905.2
2010	600.00	3566.40	10728.4	4291.4	4107.6
2011	600.00	3751.20	10779.9	4312.0	4127.3
2012	0.00	3769.20	11069.9	4428.0	4238.3
2013	0.00	3870.60	10488.2	4195.3	4015.6
2014	0.00	3667.20			

THE NET PRESENT VALUE OF THE $$ GAS @ 12.5% DISCOUNT RATE IS 15427.2

NOTES:
(1) Recorded annual placement of trash in 1000 tons.
(2) Methane generated each year in 1000 SCF per day.
(3) KW available based on (2) at a rate of 350 CFD/1000 KW
(4) Electric revenue based on (3) at $.05/kwhr, 8000 hrs/yr
(5) Annual value of gas (2) at a rate of $3.00/mmBTU

Facts didn't matter. A fact like this was recycled waste to be used for generating energy from the gas created by the garbage. A fact such as it was ADPC&E who got us in contact with the Philly operation.

Our operation didn't need to have garbage from out of state. Arkansas landfills were becoming overloaded yet our landfill sat mostly empty due to politics. The real dig in all of this was that we had started the business at the request of a politician.

The visibility our landfill was getting about Yankee Garbage didn't make sense when considering Waste Management Inc. is a national company with Yankee headquarters and operates the largest landfills in Arkansas, one located in the flood way and one too close to the airport in Little Rock. Waste Management was also running out of room at the landfill in southeast Arkansas.

Remember, it wasn't that we were looking for waste from out-of-state. It came to us though ADPC&E since we couldn't find a waste steam within the state to sustain the landfill operation.

*****

Due to the quality of the facility we began re-engineering the landfill in 1987 with as many safeguards as were known at the time. The new engineering plan called for liners, leachate collection systems and seven groundwater monitoring wells on eighty acres.

In August of 1988 we got our revised permit or modified permit. Our goal was to modify the facility to handle high volumes and offer the State of Arkansas a quality facility, setting an example for other landfills in the South.

It wasn't long before the phone started ringing from waste companies that either wanted to send us waste or purchase the landfill. We were advised by the ADPC&E that the Mitchell, Williams, Selig & Tucker Law Firm in Little Rock would be good at handling negotiations involving the landfill and to help us sort through the interested parties. So we contacted Chris Barrier with the Mitchell, Williams, Selig, & Tucker firm.

Chris was well-versed in industrial/corporate real estate transactions. We were also made aware that Alan Gates and Walter Wright, who were environmental attorneys, also worked for the Mitchell firm.

In December of 1988 we met with Michael Caulfield a lawyer representing Davenport Industries and entered into a contract to start shipping Municipal Solid Waste in the summer of 1989. This would give us the time to prepare a new cell at the landfill in preparation of the waste stream. The contract was worth over 80 million dollars over five years and that didn't include the sale of the energy from the gas.

We had no idea all the lawyer games that were going on! I was preparing the landfill for a high a volume waste stream and the State, with our same law firm, was preparing legislation to put me out of business. I want to reiterate, it was the Arkansas Dept. of Pollution Control & Ecology that suggested we take the waste from the northeast and brought the Northeasterners to our doorstep.

*****

The 1989 General Assembly was underway when we started getting information that the State was working on legislation that would limit the amount of waste a company could bring to the Arkansas landfills. The same people that had introduced us to the Northeast waste stream were now drafting legislation to stop us from receiving that waste stream?

I'll never forget going to the capital and facing a group of protesters wearing garbage bags with "No Yankee Garbage" written on both sides. The uproar was over a south Arkansas lawyer who owned a port that was going to accept and unload the Yankee waste into Arkansas landfills.

The committee gave the news as: "They will bring this Yankee trash here and don't care what the people think."

What a dumb thing to say to a bunch southern folks! An out of state company is going to dump Yankee garbage on us Southerners and turn Arkansas into a dumping ground.

There was no way that could happen based on landfill capacity in the state; nevertheless, the fear factor and the unknown, along with the words, "Yankee Garbage", had the people up in arms. It didn't matter the constitutionality of the bill proposed or that it was destined to put my company out of business. Just stop Yankee garbage.

STATE OF ARKANSAS

OFFICE OF THE ATTORNEY GENERAL

200 TOWER BUILDING

4TH & CENTER STREETS

LITTLE ROCK, ARKANSAS 72201

(501) 682-2007

STEVE CLARK
ATTORNEY GENERAL

Opinion No. 89-024

March 1, 1989

The Honorable Charlie Cole Chaffin
State Senator
Route 3, Box 1057
Benton, AR 72015

Dear Senator Chaffin:

This is in response to your request for an opinion on the constitutionality of a proposed bill to regulate the transporting and depositing of solid waste in Arkansas landfills. The bill regulates only waste transported more than one hundred miles, whether interstate or intrastate. Specifically, you are concerned primarily that the bill may violate the interstate commerce clause of the United States Constitution.

It is my opinion that the bill places an impermissible direct burden on interstate commerce, even though the seemingly evenhanded one hundred mile requirement operates to veil its discriminatory face.

In short, the regulations affect primarily interstate waste, when the legislative finding and intent evidences problems attending the transportation and disposal of all waste. It is therefore my opinion that the bill is discriminatory, places an impermissible direct burden on interstate commerce, and could definitely employ means less restrictive on interstate commerce to accomplish its purposes.

The foregoing opinion, which I hereby approve, was prepared by Assistant Attorney General Elana L. Cunningham.

Sincerely,

STEVE CLARK
Attorney General

I remember the day my wife and I were standing on the stairway waiting on Governor Clinton to leave the House of Representatives where he had been speaking. Clinton stopped as he was walking down stairs and looked at Amy, my cute little wife.

"Governor Clinton," she said and he turned and asked her name. She told him her last name was Varnadore and he wrote it down.

She looked at me after the Governor walked on. "We're screwed," she said. "He spelled our last name correctly without asking the spelling. Yep, we're screwed."

Boy howdy, she hit the nail on head.

*****

During the 1989 legislative session the task force was created. It was titled, "The Solid Waste Task Force", and Bynum Gibson was at the helm. Gibson was a top dog, hot shot attorney from Dermott, Arkansas, one of Clinton's buddies who opposed out-of-state waste and had led the march at the capital.

Not knowing much about politics, my dad and I along with my wife, Amy spent a lot of time talking to legislators. This was my first experience dealing with the legislators and with the people directly trying to put me out of business.

I remember talking to Senator Mike Beebe. At the time we were in the Senate chambers, Governor Clinton came through.

"Governor" Senator Beebe said.

Clinton stopped. "Senator Beebe?"

"Governor, I plan on running for Attorney General, and I can't vote in favor of this bill."

"Ok," Clinton said, and went on his merry way.

Senator Beebe was the only Senator that voted "NO" to the unconstitutional legislation.

*****

The State passed the legislation, Act 870, which put a two year moratorium on the importation of out-of-district waste. Despite the Attorney General Opinion, that it placed an impermissible, direct, burden on interstate commerce, the state moved forward with the legislation anyway. Continue on pg. **18.**

849.

ACT 870 1989

1 State of Arkansas   *AS ENGROSSED 3/6/89 AS ENGROSSED 3/8/89*

2 77th General Assembly   *AS ENGROSSED 3/17/89*

3 Regular Session, 1989   A Bill   HOUSE BILL

4 By: Representatives Beatty and Porter

5

6

7 For An Act To Be Entitled

8 "AN ACT TO PROVIDE FOR THE CREATION AND ESTABLISHMENT OF

9 REGIONAL SOLID WASTE PLANNING DISTRICTS AND BOARDS WHICH

10 SHALL CORRESPOND TO THE BOUNDARIES OF THE PLANNING AND

11 DEVELOPMENT DISTRICTS ESTABLISHED PURSUANT TO A.C.A.

12 §14-166-202; *TO ESTABLISH A MORATORIUM ON THE EXPANSION OF*

13 *ANY LANDFILL SERVICE AREA UNTIL JANUARY 31, 1991;* TO PROVIDE

14 THAT REGIONAL SOLID WASTE PLANNING BOARDS MUST EVALUATE THE

15 SOLID WASTE MANAGEMENT NEEDS OF THEIR AREA; AND THAT ANY

16 APPLICANT FOR A LANDFILL PERMIT UNDER A.C.A. §8-6-201, ET

17 SEQ., MUST OBTAIN A CERTIFICATE OF NEED FROM THE BOARD WITH

18 JURISDICTION OVER THE PROPOSED LANDFILL SITE; AND FOR OTHER

19 PURPOSES."

23

24 SECTION 6. *Until January 31, 1991, no existing landfill shall expand its*

25 *service area outside of the District in which it is located. Existing*

26 *landfills that currently serve areas outside of their respective Districts*

27 *shall not increase the total amount of solid waste originating from outside*

28 *their Districts by more than twenty percent (20%) of the total solid waste*

29 *received at such facility. No new landfill shall be allowed to receive solid*

30 *waste outside the boundaries of the District in which it is located until*

31 *after January 31, 1991. No new applications for landfill permits seeking to*

32 *dispose of solid waste originating outside of the district created hereunder,*

33 *or that propose to dispose of solid waste originating from outside such*

34 *district, shall be accepted or processed by the Commission or a regional solid*

35 *waste planning board, unless such applications were pending before the*

36 *Department of Pollution Control and Ecology as of March 1, 1989. All landfill*

vjf298

16

32

33 SECTION *16*. EMERGENCY. It is hereby found and determined by the

34 Seventy-Seventh General Assembly of the State of Arkansas that the current

35 system regulating solid waste in Arkansas *does not foster long-range planning*

36 *or efficient allocation of the State's solid waste resources;* that some areas

AS ENGROSSED 3/6/89   AS ENGROSSED 3/8/89   H.B.   1642

1 are facing serious shortages of capacity to the point of crisis and other

2 areas have excess capacity to the point it wastes resources; and therefore to

3 conserve precious financial resources and to avoid unnecessary land and water

4 pollution, a system of regional solid waste planning should be implemented.

5 Therefore, in order to address this serious environmental problem, an

6 emergency is hereby declared to exist, and this act being necessary for the

7 immediate preservation of the public peace, health and safety shall be in full

8 force and effect from and after its passage and approval.

9

25

26

27

28

29

30

31

32

33

34

35

36

APPROVED BY /s/ GOVERNOR

3-22-89

By the time the legislation was signed on March 22, 1989, we had a bill with the MWS&T Law Firm, according to them, of around $40,000.00. A couple of days before Governor Clinton signed the Act 870 into law, Chris Barrier called to tell me he had prepared a mortgage for $40,000.00 for their services and wanted me to come by and sign it.

We did not know at the time that MWS&T Law Firm was involved in drafting Act 870, the act that would eventually put my two companies into Chapter Eleven bankruptcy. The firm kept telling us they were working in our best interest, when in fact they should have excused themselves for having conflict of interest. They did not.

After Act 870 was signed into law, our law firm advised us to file bankruptcy, get into federal court, and get the law over turned. Still naively trusting our lying lawyers, we did file for bankruptcy. Judge Mary Davies Scott was put in charge of our case. It was just the first step in a long process we went through to overturn the legislation, ultimately too late.

*****

After six months had passed, my dad got a call about disposing of six rail car loads of sludge. I called Chris Barrier about the material and we had a new pit dug that would hold the waste. On November 7, 1989, Chris Barrier, wrote the ADPC&E and told them we planned on taking 6,000 cubic yards of dry cake sludge of non-hazardous or special waste. We gave the ADPC&E an operation plan and away we go, right? Wrong! ADPC&E had been waiting for us to make plans to receive waste into our landfill. They immediately slapped a restraining order on us.

I called Chris to informing him of the restraining order.

"Ok," he said. "You need to talk to Allen Gates or Walter Wright, so hold on and I will see if I can find one of them to help you."

In about two minutes Chris comes back on the phone.

"I don't know what to say, you need to talk to Walter Wright," he said.

"What do you mean you don't know what to say?" I questioned.

"Just talk to Walter because he's saying we can't represent you in this matter. Do what I said. Here, talk to Walter."

Walter picked up the line.

"Hey Walter, this is Gray. Chris said you and Allen couldn't represent me in this matter of the restraining order."

"No, we can't." Walter said.

"Why not," I said. "We have been waiting for an opportunity to challenge this legislation.

"Well. . . " He paused. "Allen and I drafted Act 870 and the firm would have a conflict in representing you in this matter."

I gave Walter a piece of my mind. I was livid. Walter hung up on me.

When I tried to get back to Chris I couldn't get him on the phone. Damn lawyers. Now who was going to answer this law suit? Lie and deny was what the Mitchell, Williams Selig &Tucker Firm did very well. Screw your clients. Politics is more important than integrity. (Jim Guy Tucker, a senior partner at MWS&T Firm, would resign from the law firm to become LT. Governor for the State of Arkansas, then Governor and then resigned as Governor in a world of trouble.) However, I feel they left Chris in the dark as well.

I was still in need of legal counsel and under a restraining order. The twenty days had passed before we found legal counsel to represent us and respond to the restraining order. Attorney Charles Sidney Gibson of Dermott and Russell Berry, of DeWitt, Arkansas were hired to respond to the restraining order.

The response? Because of the hold up at MWS&T the restraining order hadn't been responded to in time so because of MWS&T's strategy to keep us from challenging the state with a legitimate opportunity of winning the law suit, we lost!

I looked for a law firm later on that would sue the MWS&T Firm for malpractice. It was during the reign of Jim Guy Tucker and nobody would take the case. However, when MWS&T was pulled into bankruptcy, they went the other direction and denied ever having any interest in the facility or that we owed the firm any money. Strangely the letter below came from Allen Gates of the Mitchell Firm, wrote to me on May 14, 1991:

"In our conversation with Gray and Jeffery Treece last year (it was 1989 when they dropped us and I never had the conversation) we thought that all of us had agreed to terminate our firm's representation of you and your corporation and family members we had previously represented. It was our understanding that you had secured new legal counsel for all matters you then had pending. As we indicated in our conversation yesterday, our firm cannot represent you or any

State law hindrance to landfill, suit says

DeWitt firm sues PC&E for $64 million

DEWITT (AP) — A $64 million lawsuit filed in Arkansas County against the state Pollution Control and Ecology Department says the state's key piece of legislation controlling out-of-state garbage is unconstitutional.

The legislation was passed in 1989.

Doug Szenher, a PC&E spokesman, said his office received the 10-page complaint Monday and would have no comment until the agency's attorney has had a chance to read it.

Douglas G. Varnadore, John C. Varnadore Sr. and John C. Varnadore Jr., all of DeWitt, operators of landfill near DeWitt, filed the suit Friday in chancery court. They say the act, which limits the flow of garbage both inside the state and that which comes in from outside the state, is "an unreasonable restraint and burden on interstate commerce" and has hurt their business.

The complaint is in response to one filed by the PC&E against the Varnadores in November. At that time, the Varnadores were seeking to accept 6,000 cubic yards of sewage sludge a day from Baltimore. The PC&E asked for and received a temporary restraining order against the company until the agency had time to review the Varnadores' plans.

Since then, the Varnadores, doing business as Southeast Arkansas Landfill Inc., asked the PC&E for permission to accept waste from Fayetteville. In an April 6 letter, the PC&E denied the request, saying that a part of the 1989 act says that "until January 31, 1991, no existing landfill shall expand its service area outside of the district in which it is located.

"Existing landfills that currently serve areas outside of their respective districts shall not increase the total amount of solid waste originating from outside their districts by more than ... 20 percent of the total solid waste received as such facility."

The Varnadores say that those districts are arbitrary.

Charles Sidney Gibson, attorney for the landfill company, said the loss of the Fayetteville business had not been included in the suit but would be argued in court. He said that the Varnadores had been trying to work with the PC&E but had filed the suit because a landfill in Little Rock, which handles a large amount of garbage, was allowed to take the Fayetteville waste. Gibson said the Little Rock landfill has less capacity than the Varnadores' landfill.

The landfill company, the complaint says, has spent a great deal of money to design and operate a landfill that is environmentally sound. By limiting what the landfill can accept, the PC&E is hindering the company from making profits to pay off its debts, the suit says.

Gibson said the law was passed in the hysteria of trying to stop the flow of out-of-state waste and that no thought was given to the effects the law would have on the development of landfills in the state.

At a glance

■ 1989 law limits the flow of garbage inside the state and that which comes in from outside.

■ In November, the landfill company sought to accept 6,000 cubic yards of sewage sludge a day from Baltimore.

■ The PC&E asked for and received a temporary restraining order against the company.

member of your family, or any of your business entities at the present time. To avoid any confusion at this point we will file a notice of withdrawal as counsel in this case no. E-89-114." That letter came later in 1991, and the incident occurred in 1989.

This was what we had previously received in 1989:

Promissory Note for the sum of $40,000: "Promissory Note, Guaranty Agreement, Security Agreement, and Stock Pledge" document of March 15, 1989 for the sum of $40,000. In effect, a retainer for attorney fees paid by Gray to MWS&T to represent him and Arkansas County Waste Inc. secured by "certain interest in real estate in Arkansas County owned by D. Gray Varnadore as an heir to the Toland Estate" plus property and stock in S.E.A.L. Inc. on 23, March, 1989, a "Mortgage" document was filed securing the property to MWS&T. In the 1991 letter they said they had dropped represented us before the Act 870 and held no interest in our businesses and we owed them no money? Strange.

*****

In the fall of 1990 we were preparing for the next legislative session to begin in January of 1991. I wrote Governor Clinton a letter about allowing the moratorium to expire. Clinton wrote me back, (letter pg.) simply saying that he didn't know how to help my companies. That let me know what I was going to be facing in the next session. With two companies in bankruptcy and my parents forced to live on their social security, I was ready for the next session.

Not being able to bring waste in from other parts of the state, much less take waste from out-of-state had nothing to do with the operation of the landfill or the hauling company. The moratorium restricted me from going outside of a ten county area to seek a waste stream from the areas that Waste Management already had a monopoly on.

The waste stream I was pursuing was recycled and more bio-degradable than the small amount of local waste that was coming to the facility. The charge for local waste was at $5.50 per yard and the recycled out-of-state waste I was looking to receive was $43.50 per yard. The cost of waste disposal in the northeast United States was in excess of $45.00 per yard.

So what would you do? Look for a more profitable waste stream that's clean, recycled and make a profit or continue being dominated by the politicians playing Waste Management and

STATE OF ARKANSAS
OFFICE OF THE GOVERNOR
State Capitol
Little Rock 72201

Bill Clinton
Governor

December 19, 1990

Gray Varnadore
310 East Cross Street
Dewitt, AR   72042

Dear Gray:

I understand you have contacted my office regarding the impact Act 870 of 1989 has had on your solid waste business. Although you may not agree, Act 870 reflects the collective concern and interest the legislature, citizens of the state, and I have for managing solid waste, particularly within the region waste originates. Act 870 was passed to give the state time to plan and to develop regional solutions to our solid waste problems. In conversations with hundreds of people this past year, no strong disagreement with Act 870 surfaced except from those that believed the state should have passed stronger legislation dealing with out of district waste.

Gray, I am not aware any solution to your specific problem that would not put the state in the same position it found itself in prior to the 1989 legislative session. Thank you for contacting my office.

Sincerely,

Bill Clinton

BC:ks:md

stay in bankruptcy? When your government breaks you on purpose and wants to keep you down to give your competitor a monopoly, because they contribute large sums of money and play the political games, you'd be ready for the fight too.

*****

By the time the 78th legislative session started, I had already been in contact with Star Recycling of Brooklyn, New York. They were interested in sending recycled waste to the landfill. They flew me to New York to see their facility.

The Star Recycling facility was in down town Brooklyn. It looked to be two blocks in size and had an eight foot, chain link fence around the whole facility. It had Geiger counters at the gate and all the waste went into the building for recycling.

It had hand picking operations on three separate conveyors and the facility was incredible clean. They had monitors that watched every inch of the facility. I've never been to, nor seen a recycling facility that was so well operated and clean. Every piece of waste had a place and they were very particular about their waste stream.

Allowing the moratorium to expire would be the saving grace for our landfill. There would be a good consistent waste stream for the facility and at a price we might even make a dollar. I was keeping my fingers crossed that the moratorium would be lifted.

However, once again State Rep. Bynum Gibson was leading the crusade to extend the moratorium for another two years, even though it was only my business that was being affected. The big guys were not being affected at all.

Rep. Gibson dove right in with both feet expecting for this moratorium extension bill, to be approved by the committee the first time through. This time the other State House Reps. understood and realized it's not up to them to oversee the operation of the landfills. That was ADPC&E's job and if the waste is acceptable to go into the landfill and there are no operational issues then the waste should be accepted. We had no operational issues, only the restricted, illegal legislation, but then everything turned to politics. The January 23, 1991 news articles give a full run down of my situation. Continue on pg. **30.**

The 78th General Assembly

Longer halt on out-of-state trash opposed

By Caroline Decker
Gazette Staff

A landfill operator Tuesday denounced a bill that would extend a moratorium limiting the amount of garbage a landfill can accept from outside district boundaries.

"The moratorium ... has actually put our landfill in a Chapter 11 [bankruptcy] situation, unable to accept materials from outside our district," Gray Varnadore, president of South East Arkansas Landfill Inc. in De-Witt, told the House Public Health, Welfare and Labor Committee.

If the moratorium is extended, Varnadore said, his family-owned landfill business "absolutely" would fold.

Varnadore filed bankruptcy because the southeast district in which his operation is located did not generate enough business to keep his landfill profitable, he said.

The southeast district and seven other districts were established by the General Assembly in 1989 as Arkansas's eight regional solid waste planning districts.

To compete effectively with the four other landfills in his district, Varnadore said, he relied heavily on out-of-district waste.

The South East Arkansas Landfill accepts 10 tons of waste from within its district each day. Varnadore said that to break even, the landfill would need to accept between 250 and 300 tons each day.

The current moratorium, approved by the legislature in 1989, expires Jan. 31. Rep. Bynum Gibson of Dermott wants to extend the out-of-district garbage limit until July 1, 1992, or until landfills in the state reach a 10-year capacity. Currently, the state's 63 existing municipal landfills have landfill life of just over four years.

Gibson said extending the moratorium would give the districts more time to develop regional solid waste management solutions.

Under the current moratorium, existing landfills can accept out-of-district and out-of-state waste if the volume and weight do not exceed more than 20 percent of the total waste

File Photo
Bynum Gibson: Dermott representative wants to extend the out-of-district garbage limit until July 1, 1992.

received each year.

Varnadore said that he could receive up to two tons of additional waste each day under the moratorium. The extra waste would bring only an additional $25 a day, he said.

Varnadore would be in the "black" except that the moratorium prohibited his company from accepting a contract to bury waste from the cities of Kingsport, Pa., and Fayetteville, he said.

Varnadore filed a lawsuit against the state in October, challenging the moratorium on the grounds that it impeded interstate commerce. The lawsuit asks for a temporary restraining order against the moratorium.

ARKANSAS DEMOCRAT ● WEDNESDAY, JANUARY 23, 1991

Landfill owner cites harm of moratorium, opposes extension

BY DON JOHNSON
Democrat Staff Writer

A bill that would extend the current moratorium on out-of-state waste has drawn opposition from one landfill owner who says the law has placed his firm in bankruptcy.

House Bill 1169 will be considered by the House Public Health, Welfare and Labor Committee on Thursday. Without the legislation, the moratorium adopted in 1989 will be lifted at the end of January.

The other elements of Gov. Bill Clinton's environmental package will be considered by the committee on Feb. 5.

D. Gray Varnadore said his company, Southeast Arkansas Landfill Inc. of DeWitt (Arkansas County), has been forced into Chapter 11 bankruptcy because of the restrictions.

Varnadore said his landfill was accepting 10 tons of waste a day in 1989 when the law was passed. Since the moratorium, Varnadore's company can only accept an additional 2 tons of waste outside a certain area.

The area is based on the economic development district in Southeast Arkansas.

He said his company must receive 250 to 300 tons of waste a day to make a profit.

The DeWitt landfill is one of five in the district. Varnadore said the district is dominated by Pine Bluff Waste Disposal, which is owned by Waste Management Inc.

"The quality landfills are unable to receive enough ma-

See LANDFILL, Page 4

Landfill

● Continued from Page 1

terials to stay open," he said.

Varnadore said the law creates landfills in areas that are not suitable for them. He said an extension of the law would mean other landfills would go out of business.

Rep. Bynum Gibson of Dermott, sponsor of the bill, said he wasn't aware of Varnadore's situation and hadn't heard of any other objections from landfill owners.

Gibson said he didn't believe the bill would be controversial.

25

The 78th General Assembly

Landfill moratorium not extended

Don Marquis/Gazette Staff

DISAPPOINTED: Rep. Bynum Gibson listens to debate about his landfill bill which the Public Health, Welfare and Labor Committee deferred Thursday.

Bill would have banned trash 2½ more years

By Caroline Decker
Gazette Staff

A legislative committee Thursday rejected a bill to extend a 1989 moratorium that bans landfills from accepting out-of-district garbage, a move that could jeopardize the governor's package of solid waste bills and open up Arkansas landfills to accept "Yankee" trash.

"If you have a huge influx of out-of-state waste and a huge transfer within the state ... it will destroy any regional [solid waste] plan in the state," said Rep. Bynum Gibson of Dermott, whose bill proposed to extend the moratorium until July 1, 1992.

Currently, the state's landfill capacity is critically low. Its 63 municipal landfills will be usable for just over more four years.

Extending the moratorium would give the state time to develop regional solutions to solid waste problems and increase landfill capacity to 10 years, Gibson said.

The Public Health, Welfare and Labor Committee voted to defer a decision to extend the moratorium until Feb. 5, when it will consider other solid waste legislation.

The current moratorium is set to expire Jan. 31, but Rep. Bobby Tullis of Mineral Springs scrambled to introduce a bill into the House on Thursday that would extend the trash ban for 30 days. The extension would buy time for lawmakers to consider the impact of continuing the moratorium for another 2½ years.

If Tullis' bill does not pass in the House or Senate, and does not get Gov. Bill Clinton's signature by Jan. 31, the moratorium would expire, leaving the state Department of Pollution Control and Ecology free to issue permits for landfills to accept out-of-district and out-of-state waste.

Clinton said Thursday that he was disappointed the committee didn't pass Gibson's bill, but indicated that any problems could be worked out.

"I don't think the legislature wants to be on the record as opening the state of Arkansas to an unlimited flood of out-of-state garbage 30 days from now," Clinton said.

"The committee is saying that we need greater flexibility [for transporting waste within the state]," he said.

Clinton would not say Thursday whether he would sign a bill to extend the moratorium for 30 days.

Gray Varnadore, president of South East Arkansas Landfill Inc. in DeWitt, testified before the committee that the moratorium had forced his company to file for bankruptcy. In 1988, Varnadore spent $300,000 to upgrade the family-owned landfill and had planned to accept trash from Fayetteville and Pennsylvania, he said.

When the moratorium passed in 1989, Varnadore said he was forced to give up the out-of-district contracts.

In 1989, the General Assembly divided the state into eight regional solid waste planning districts. Under the 1989 moratorium, landfills already importing out-of-district and out-of-state waste could continue to do so, if weight and volume of such waste did not exceed 20 percent of the total waste received each year.

South East Arkansas Landfill, which competes with four other landfills within its district, brings in 10 tons of waste each day, Varnadore said. The landfill needs 250 to 300 tons a day to turn a profit, he said. Under the moratorium, Varnadore's landfill can accept only an additional two tons of waste each day from outside district boundaries.

In October, Varnadore filed suit against the state, challenging the moratorium on the grounds that it impeded interstate commerce and prevented him from honoring contracts to municipalities outside his district. A hearing is set for Feb. 6.

Rep. Sturgis Miller of Pine Bluff warned that allowing Varnadore to accept waste from other districts would violate federal regulations. It is unconstitutional to limit transportation of out-of-state waste unless the transportation of in-state waste also is restricted, he said.

Recycling measures are rolling

Panel favors extending garbage ban

BY DON JOHNSON
Democrat Staff Writer

During a special meeting Friday, the House Public Health, Welfare and Labor Committee endorsed a bill extending for 30 days a moratorium on garbage imports.

The special meeting became necessary after the committee on Thursday deferred action until Feb. 5 on House Bill 1169 by Rep. Bynum Gibson of Dermott.

HB 1169 would have extended the moratorium on landfills accepting garbage from other areas of the state or outside the state.

The current moratorium ends Jan. 31 and Gibson's bill would have extended it for two years or until the state's landfill capacity had more than doubled.

Rep. Bobby Tullis of Mineral Springs, who made the motion to delay consideration of Gibson's bill, introduced the measure Thursday to extend the moratorium until March 2 and asked for a special committee meeting.

Tullis said he hoped the House would pass the bill by Monday or Tuesday.

Tullis had asked that Gibson introduce a 30-day extension, but Gibson declined, saying such a proposal was "silly."

JoEllen Black/Gazette Staf

ON THEIR SIDE: Gov. Bill Clinton gestures to one of his representatives across the House Public Health, Welfare and Labor Committee room Thursday to show his support for Rep. Bynum Gibson's package of solid waste bills.

Gov. Bill Clinton said Friday he was inclined to support Tullis' bill, saying it was a "good-faith effort to buy some time."

Gibson's bill extending the moratorium is part of Clinton's legislative package.

HB 1169 will be considered by the committee on Feb. 5 with other solid waste legislation.

Tullis told the committee he offered the bill so there wouldn't be a gap in the moratorium.

"You can vote however you want to (on Feb. 5), but we can't have a gap," Tullis said.

In 1989, the Legislature approved a bill establishing eight regional solid waste planning districts. Existing landfills could accept only a certain amount of out-of-state and out-of-district garbage.

Tullis said he did not want out-of-state garbage flooding the state, but wanted more time to review Gibson's bill.

Northwest Arkansas legislators are concerned about

Trash problem plagues state

If the legislature extends its moratorium restricting the movement of trash in the state, northwest Arkansas residents could find themselves without a landfill in about a year, said a Department of Pollution Control and Ecology official.

Of the three landfills in the northwest district, two (Fulton Sanitation in Benton County and Sunray in Washington County) have nearly reached capacity and may close in a year, said Tom Boston, chief of PC&E's solid waste division. The third, in Baxter County, is privately owned and not obligated to accept garbage from anyone, he said.

The Sunray Company has submitted a pre-application to open a landfill in Washington County, but the site has received public opposition.

The northwest district is not well suited for landfills because of its poor geography, said Harry Elliott, enforcement coordinator for PC&E's solid waste division.

If a new landfill is not permitted before the others close, the district could contract with the private landfill in Baxter County. But it might be too expensive to haul garbage the 100 miles from Fayetteville to Baxter County, Boston said. The district's other option is to haul waste across the Missouri and Oklahoma borders.

But both states are considering legislation that would limit out-of-state waste, Boston said.

The February 8, 1991 picture of Governor Clinton is gesturing that he is in favor of extending the landfill moratorium bill that Rep. Bynum Gibson was trying to get approved. At that point Rep. Bynum Gibson was unable to get the bill passed. The look on Bynum's face when he couldn't get the bill passed and out of committee was shock. This went on in both the House and the Senate committee through out the month of February.

Most everybody in the House and Senate realized the bill was unconstitutional and had put my companies out of business. It is not the plan of the state representatives to put landfills and waste companies out of business. Finally, I had them understanding my dilemma and Senator Charlie Cole Chaffin was working with us to keep the moratorium from being extended. Then Clinton and I had a few words.

THE BILL CLINTON AND GRAY EXCHANGE AT THE CAPITAL

On Tuesday, February 19th, 1991 there was a sub-committee meeting for the environmental issues concerning the moratorium extension. I had been talking to House Representative Bobby Tullis about an amendment to the bill that would allow us, with upgraded engineering, to be exempt from the moratorium. During our conversation Governor Bill Clinton entered the sub-committee room.

"Governor," Tullis called out. Clinton turned and came to where Tullis and I were standing. "I am considering an amendment to the moratorium bill, which would allow landfills with up-graded engineering to receive more—"Tullis started.

"I'll veto it!" Clinton interrupted, then turned away and walked to the door.

I caught the door before it shut and walked into the hall to catch up with the Governor as he walked away.

"Governor," I said. He kept walking as if he didn't hear me. "Governor!" I said again and by now I was walking beside him. We were stride for stride. No response. "Governor Clinton, can I—"

"You're interrupting my day!" He turned to me and screamed, not a yell but a scream, in my face as if he was having a temper tantrum. Clinton's nose was less than an inch from my face and he was screaming, "You're interrupting my day!"

As he glared at me, his eyes were red and swollen, with his nose still less than inch from my face. "I can't walk in the hall without being interrupted by you!"

"Interrupting your day?" I screamed back. "You've interrupted my life. I have two companies in bankruptcy and my mother and father forced to live on social security because of you. (Clinton, wanting to extend the moratorium for two more years.)

"I sympathize with you," Clinton said.

"I don't want your sympathy. I want to operate my business," I replied.

We were still pretty much nose to nose, glaring at one another when I realized that one of the Governor's advisors had grabbed one of my arms and was trying to pull me away from him. No such luck. I stood there until Clinton turned and walked away from me.

The Governor looked back over his shoulder and said, "I'll do everything I can to keep you from bringing in Yankee garbage. Our poll showed 93 percent of the voting public is against out-of-state garbage, and the other 7 percent didn't respond."

"This issue doesn't have to be about out-of-state waste," I said. "Right now Waste Management collects garbage from our county and takes it back to Pine Bluff where their landfill is located. The landfill at Shannon Road has been sited by State Geologist Tony Morris as the most polluting landfill that Waste Management operates in Arkansas."

Clinton slowed down, turned toward me, and said, "You're interrupting my day." Clinton screamed at me again as he turned to walk away from me. "I'm not handling the waste issue. I'm letting other groups handle it."

"Sure, groups like Waste Management, BFI, and Sunray, who are contributing thousands to your campaign." I said. "You're not concerned about the environment. All you're concerned about is contributions and building a larger national base because you're going to run for President."

Clinton stopped in his tracks. He turned directly toward me. He was mad. I might as well have pissed on his foot.

"You're interrupting my day!" He screamed, as he came back to get nose to nose with me again. His adviser was pulling harder on my arm. What was with this same statement? Interrupting his day? "You don't know what you're talking about," Clinton screamed. "Get out of here and quit interrupting me."

"No." I replied. "Not until you tell me what I have to do to get this amendment Okayed so I can get my companies back in business."

"You get my attorneys to agree to the amendment," Clinton said.

"You control what your attorneys agree to." I said

At that point Clinton's advisers were pulling on him as well as me. I stepped back and turned to see who was pulling on my arm. It was Phil Wasson; a **liaison** Clinton had working during the session. I decided to walk away from this futile argument and noticed that our confrontation had attracted the usual crowd of gawkers.

People had poured into the hallways to surround us and others were watching from office doorways. A reporter with the AP (Ron Fornnhia) approached me. "Do you have a comment?" he asked.

Fuck him!!

"I can't print that," the reporter said.

"I don't care what you print. Clinton's not concerned about the environmental issues. He's just concerned about keeping his contributors happy."

"It didn't sound as if the Governor was in favor of your amendment," Ron continued.

"All he has on his mind is raising taxes and running for president. That's why he's letting Waste Management dictate policy. He wants the backing of their large national base and their billion dollar annual revenue. Who cares that Waste Management is running the worst landfill in the Arkansas. He's just looking at how many votes and how much money his so-called policies will bring him."

"Why would Waste Management want to extend the moratorium?" Ron asked.

"Waste Management controls a great deal of the material and landfills in the Northeast. Disposal prices in the Northeast range from 38 dollars to 63 dollars per yard. Waste Management doesn't want to lose that high dollar waste stream. They already have a monopoly on the waste in our district."

"Do you think the Governor will change his mind about your amendment?"

"If he were a true Governor, yes. He'd require our district to utilize our open, empty facility. But Clinton? He's a pecker head with a title and has much higher ambitions."

I didn't have a lot to say to the reporter. I was angry and stunned over what just occurred. I headed home. I'd go back to DeWitt and come back Thursday and try again.

When I arrived at the capital Thursday for the committee meeting, I found out that our ally, Senator Chaffin, had a talk with Clinton after my confrontation. Suddenly she took the Senate version of the House moratorium bill, on Wednesday, ran it through the Senate then to the House and it was a done deal by the time I returned, waiting for Clinton's signature. The moratorium had been extended.

We had been sold out and for what? Senator Charlie Cole Chaffin traded us for triple beams. That's right, triple beam scales that were confiscated in drug raids and she was donating to chemistry classes. Lie, lie, and lie! She should have been a lawyer instead of a chemistry teacher and now Senator. It still fits the political roll of, "you can't trust a politician."

*****

Clinton was victorious, once again. The moratorium was extended regardless of my efforts to keep it from happening. Nevertheless, I had plans to start off loading baled, recycled waste in March of 1992 and hoped in the meantime that Judge Mary Davies Scott would overturn the moratorium.

I made arrangements to lease a rail spur in Stuttgart, Arkansas. I was also preparing a new cell to put the waste in and get equipment to handle the waste stream. I was getting ready for the waste stream and I was keeping ADPC&E Solid Waste Chief, Tom Boston, aware of my every move.

The State law required a permit for a transfer station when waste is taken from a smaller truck and transferred to a larger truck. We were going from the larger rail car to the smaller 18 wheeler so no permit for that was required.

The state didn't require landfills to weigh material. If they didn't have scales, they were to determine the size by the square yard. That worked for me. I didn't have to weigh the waste nor did I have to have a transfer permit. The only thing that they had to stop me was this unconstitutional law. Continue on pg. **41.**

The 78th General Assembly

Waste management is such a nasty business

Ernest Dumas

Garbage is a nasty and cut-throat business, though you would never know it by its civilized legislative battles.

The Public Health, Welfare and Labor Committee of the House of Representatives will take up the pivotal part of Gov. Bill Clinton's big solid-waste program today. It would establish a system of landfills regulated by regional authorities, enabling big and small cities and counties to meet the tough new government rules for disposing of their wastes.

Big national waste companies think the legislation would knock them out of a lucrative market. It wouldn't, but the state wouldn't be a feeding pen for them.

With luck and a lift from Clinton, who has been an indifferent father of the waste and recycling reforms at times, the bill may get a favorable recommendation from the House committee and perhaps even pass the House, although that looks problematic.

In the Senate, say its foes, it is certainly dead. The legislation has an energetic sponsor in the House, Rep. Bynum Gibson of Dermott, who has given it his single-minded attention. In the other chamber, Sen. Jack Gibson of Dermott, who also was a member of the task force that drafted the sweeping strategy, has had other fish to fry, mainly a highway program.

The legislation has few but mighty opponents: the two titans in the waste business in the United States and Arkansas Power and Light Co.

AP&L doesn't lose legislative battles, big or small. Last week, it got exempted from a state recycling fee levied on on-site industrial landfills, but it and the electric cooperatives would play an almost indispensable role in the waste management districts. They would collect garbage fees for the regional authorities through monthly electric bills.

AP&L and the cooperatives don't like being pack horses for the government, although as monopolies enjoying a little government protection they have a little heavier burden of citizenship. The power companies collect taxes for local governments already.

There is no other way to collect garbage fees from everyone who contributes to the waste stream in Arkansas except through electric bills. Nearly everyone is an electric customer.

Although collecting the fee would cost the companies nothing, they and the cooperatives believe that they would absorb the consumer resentment.

The big waste companies have more at stake: monopolization of the growing waste market. Solid waste management is one of the nation's growth industries. Communities everywhere are running out of places to deposit their garbage and the companies have landfills.

Waste Management, Inc., is the largest company in the $30

billion solid waste industry. Browning Ferris Industries (BFI) is not too far behind. Both have been nailing down contracts with Arkansas cities to collect and dispose of their garbage.

You'd expect garbage to be a seamy business, and it is. Penalties and fines are almost a standard part of the cost of doing business in an industry where turf wars get mean.

All across the country, Waste Management and BFI have been charged and fined for violations of pollution laws, for price-fixing and for other conspiracies. The Justice Department, the Environmental Protection Agency and the Securities and Exchange Commission have gotten after them.

Waste Management says many of its legal troubles arose from companies that it took over and that such problems have ended.

Greenpeace, the militant environmental group, published a summary of Waste Management's legal troubles in 1986. It compiled a total of $31 million in fines and settlements. There have been more since then. Subsidiaries of Waste Management and BFI pled guilty to price-fixing in the Toledo area and agreed to pay a $1 million fine.

Last year, the two companies settled a class-action suit in the federal District Court for the Eastern District of Pennsylvania alleging that they had conspired to fix prices in communities across the country. One of them was Crittenden County, Ark.

Waste Management agreed to pay $19.5 million and BFI $30.5 million. They insisted that they had done nothing wrong but settled to bring an end to the expense and distraction of the lawsuit.

They are savvy negotiators, in court or at city hall. The solid-waste authorities would level the playing field for local communities. Without them, the companies will eventually divide up the state — legally.

Ernest Dumas is an associate editor for the Arkansas Gazette.

SAFECO LAND TITLE

Crime/Courts

ARKANSAS DEMOCRAT • FRIDAY, AUGUST 2, 1991

Judge ponders constitutionality of waste moratorium

BY LARRY AULT
Democrat Staff Writer

A federal judge Thursday began deliberating whether a state law that a businessman claims forced him into bankruptcy should be struck down as unconstitutional.

U.S. Bankruptcy Judge Mary Davies Scott heard two days of testimony in a bankruptcy-related lawsuit that alleged the Legislature's moratorium on out-of-state waste forcedGray Varnadore of DeWitt (Arkansas County) into bankruptcy.

If Scott rules in favor of Varnadore, five years of efforts by state pollution control officials may have been wasted.

Varnadore alleged his Southeast Arkansas Landfill Inc. was forced into Chapter 11 bankruptcy this year by state landfill laws. The moratorium was put into effect in 1989. It divided the state into eight regions and placed limits on how much trash can be transported between the regions. Limited out-of-state trash was a side-effect of the legislation.

The Legislature this year extended the temporary moratorium two years and added more regional landfill boards that have more authority to regulate solid waste.

Landfill moratorium ineffective, discriminatory, attorney says

By Caroline Decker
Gazette Staff

A lawyer for a bankrupt southeast Arkansas landfill operator contended in federal court Thursday that a moratorium limiting the movement of garbage did little to force the state's eight regional solid waste districts to deal with their garbage problems.

The moratorium's restriction on the movement of garbage into the state and across district lines is directed toward landfill operators, not generators of the waste, contended Charles Sidney Gibson of Dermott, attorney for Gray Varnadore of DeWitt.

Gibson said the law unfairly discriminated against the amount of out-of-district garbage that landfill operators could accept without directly limiting where cities and counties could dispose of trash.

Steve Weaver, attorney for the state Pollution Control and Ecology Department, defended the moratorium, saying it was necessary to implement regional garbage pick-up and disposal plans statewide.

The state legislature adopted the moratorium in 1989 to force regional waste districts to get a handle on the amount of garbage generated in each district and assess the need for additional landfill space.

State officials contended that districts could not assess their own garbage needs when unlimited amounts of trash could freely move into and throughout the state.

At the time the moratorium took effect, out-of-state waste amounted to 4 percent of all the garbage buried in Arkansas landfills, Randall Mathis, state Pollution Control and Ecology director, told the court. Mathis said he knew of no alternatives that would put pressure on solid waste districts to develop regional garbage plans.

Mathis also told the court that he did not know how allowing Varnadore to accept out-of-state waste would thwart the state's efforts to develop regional garbage disposal plans.

The legislature recently extended the moratorium until July 1992 or until the state has a 10-year landfill capacity. Under the current moratorium, landfill operators can accept 50 tons of out-of-district garbage daily or can increase by 20 percent the amount of garbage it accepts from outside sources based on the total amount of trash a landfill accepted in January 1989.

moratorium restrictions that limit the transfer of garbage between the solid waste districts, Tullis said.

Landfill capacity in the Northwest Arkansas district is declining. Tullis said more flexibility was needed in transferring garbage between the state districts.

Gibson said an end to the moratorium could result in landfills accepting garbage from other areas of the state or from out of state. If that occurred, he said the state's landfill capacity, which is already too low, could be reduced even further.

Landfill operator wants moratorium on garbage lifted

The Associated Press

PINE BLUFF — A bankrupt landfill operator is challenging Arkansas' moratorium on out-of-state garbage.

Steve Weaver, chief counsel with the state Pollution Control and Ecology Department, said the state's borders would be opened to a flood of garbage from East Coast states if Arkansas loses. The suit names the PC&E as the defendant.

"This is one of the more important cases for us this year," Weaver said. "If the moratorium is lifted all that control is gone. Local governments will be victim to whatever waste stream an entrepreneur can generate."

Federal Bankruptcy Judge Mary Davies Scott will hear the case of Gray Varnadore on July 31 at Little Rock.

"The constitutionality of these laws is up in the air," said Varnadore's lawyer, Charles Sidney Gibson of Dermott.

Varnadore's landfill business, Southeast Arkansas Landfill Inc. in DeWitt, went bankrupt last year.

Varnadore says the state is violating federal Interstate Commerce law. His complaint relies on U.S. Supreme Court and U.S. Court of Appeals decisions that say moving solid waste from state to state can't be restricted, said Varnadore's bankruptcy lawyer, Jeff Treece of Little Rock.

The Legislature in 1989 voted to stop the importation of solid waste and created solid waste districts to avoid violating the Interstate Commerce law. The Legislature passed a law that said garbage could not cross district boundaries or the state's boundaries.

State officials said Arkansas is not violating Interstate Commerce laws, because the state has the same restrictions on garbage from out of state as it does for garbage from inside the state.

> 'The only way they can win is if they can characterize it as a ban.'

"I feel fairly comfortable there is not an out-of-state waste ban in this state, and they are trying to make it one," Weaver said. "The only way they can win is if they can characterize it as a ban."

A federal appeals court upheld a Michigan law that said a county could ban waste from outside its borders because the county restricted in-state garbage no differently from the way it restricted out-of-state garbage, Weaver said.

The matter may come down to whether Arkansas' moratorium is "discriminatory on its face," in its disregard for garbage as a privileged item of interstate commerce, lawyers for both sides said.

Tuesday, August 6, 1991   Arkansas Gazette

Pine Bluff landfill exceeds legal limit

By Caroline Decker
Gazette Staff

Overfilling a landfill in Pine Bluff is going to cost Waste Management Inc. $104,000.

Waste Management, the world's largest waste-hauling and disposal company, has had too much garbage in its Shannon Road landfill for about a year, said Tom Boston, chief of the solid waste division of the state Department of Pollution Control and Ecology. In some areas, the landfill is 9 feet above its permitted height, he said.

Laura Mack, a PC&E attorney, said Waste Management had agreed to pay the fine or conduct an environmental project at that cost for the department. A possible project would be assessing the water quality of the Ouachita River.

A landfill packed with too much trash adds additional weight to a landfill's liner and can make it more susceptible to leaks, said Tony Morris, a geologist with the department's solid waste division.

PC&E officials, in separate interviews, said they thought the Shannon Road landfill was leaking.

"In my opinion, the data indicates there is a problem," Morris said. Samples taken from groundwater monitoring wells nearby have high levels of iron, chlorides and sulfates, which are an indicator of a leaky landfill, he said.

Test results indicated the landfill may have been leaking for about 18 months, Boston said. However, the landfill is not situated near any wells used for drinking water or for agriculture, he said.

"There doesn't appear to be any significant levels of harm," Boston said.

Mary Drake, an attorney for Waste Management in Dallas, said the company had admitted to overfilling the landfill, but disputed PC&E's test results that indicated the landfill was leaking.

In January, 1992 Judge Mary Davies Scott failed to overturn the moratorium, so now we had to file an appeal to her ruling. The appeal landed in Federal Judge Steven Reasoner court. That wasn't any better. Most every legal person we talked to couldn't believe that this law wasn't found illegal. But, it is in Arkansas and Governor Bill Clinton was running for President of the United States. Donations took front seat over legalities.

By the way in our 1991 confrontation, I told Clinton I knew he was running for President and that Waste Management was one of his biggest backers. It hit a nerve because he had told the people of Arkansas if he was elected Governor a second time, he would not run for another office until his term concluded. Another lie? I think that conversation put the nails in my business coffin.

*****

I still had plans to start taking waste from Star Recycling in1992. We had filed an appeal to the Eight Circuit Court of Appeals, in St Louis to overthrow the Act 870 but it wasn't set for a hearing until August of 1992.

In February I had the landfill ready and the equipment needed to do the job. We were working on the offloading dock, inclosing it so waste wouldn't blow around. Getting a Bob Cat with forks long enough to pick-up the bales was a challenge, but everything and everybody on my team was ready and waiting on the first car to arrive.

In March 17, 1992 the first rail car arrived. It was just what they said it would be. Gene, my employee that I put in charge of offloading the waste, jumped right to work. He had the first load ready to go to the landfill in about forty-five minutes.

It worked very well. Each rail car was four trucks loads. We hauled the waste by enclosed van trailer to the landfill pulled the material out and headed back to the rail spur. This went on for three weeks without a glitch, until some kids came over to the rail spur to look at the graffiti that was painted on the box car. "New York Garbage Shipped to DeWitt"

"Nasty stench in Stuttgart at rail spur!" The April, 22, 1992 news articles proclaimed. You can read to see how the news media put their own little spin on, "Yankee Garbage."

I remember one morning when it first hit the newspaper, my phone rang. Continue on pg. **48.**

State holds its nose as Brooklyn garbage piles up near Stuttgart

BY RACHEL O'NEAL
Democrat-Gazette Capitol Bureau

The importation of out-of-state garbage is raising a stink in Arkansas County, state officials said Tuesday.

Larry Wilson, deputy director of the state Department of Pollution Control and Ecology, said the owner of a landfill apparently is creating an odor nuisance by storing hundreds of tons of solid waste in Stuttgart before taking it to a DeWitt landfill. The waste is shipped from Brooklyn, N.Y.

"I'm concerned because I don't know what's in the waste," Lt. Gov. Jim Guy Tucker said Tuesday. "I'm concerned because as much as 150 tons of garbage stored in boxcars is sitting in Stuttgart.

"But most of all, I am concerned that there does not appear to be any public hearing on this," Tucker said.

The company was required to hold a public hearing and apply to PC&E for a permit modification before accepting the waste, Wilson said.

"The people in Arkansas County and people in the state have a right to know and a right to ask questions before hundreds of tons of Brooklyn garbage is brought into Arkansas."

The waste is being shipped by rail from New York to Southeast Arkansas Landfill Inc.

Between three to four boxcars of solid waste arrives each week. The waste is kept in boxcars for up to a week before it is taken to DeWitt, Wilson said.

Wilson added that about 42 tons of waste is moved from the boxcars to the landfill each day. Under state law, a landfill cannot dispose of more than 50 tons of waste per day, he said.

D. Gray Varnadore, who operates the landfill, said Tuesday he has a permit for dispos-

See GARBAGE, Page 11A

42

Garbage

● Continued from Page One

ing out-of-state waste.

"There is nothing in my permit that says I have to hold a public hearing," Varnadore said.

Varnadore added that one company handles 95 percent of the waste in Southeast Arkansas.

"If we could get garbage from in-state, we would not be accepting it from out of state. But we either receive garbage from outside our district or go under."

Varnadore has run into problems with PC&E in the past. In November 1991 the state obtained a temporary restraining order preventing a train dubbed the "poo-poo choo-choo" from disposing of a 12,000-ton load of Maryland sewer sludge in Varnadore's landfill.

Varnadore filed for protection from his creditors in October 1990 under Chapter 11 of the federal bankruptcy code. He later said state laws limiting out-of-state waste placed his company in bankruptcy.

Varnadore said Southeast Arkansas Landfill is still in bankruptcy. But he said his other company, Arkansas Waste Services, which unloads the garbage from the railroad cars, is not in bankruptcy.

PC&E learned about the current situation when residents of a Stuttgart mobile home park complained about the odor, Wilson said.

"One of the concerns we have is we aren't sure what is being sent here," Wilson said. "In two inspections, we've seen no evidence of household hazardous waste, but we have seen some items that might have been medical waste."

PC&E recently contacted Brooklyn officials and learned the solid waste had been stripped of materials that can be recycled, Wilson said.

PC&E inspectors then examined the trash and found some items that probably are medical waste, including plastic tubing, rubber gloves and bags that contained soft food, Wilson said.

"We had offloaded up there for over a month and there wasn't an odor problem until the trailer park residents found out the garbage was coming from out of state," Varnadore said.

On April 17, PC&E sent a notice of violation to Varnadore. The notice asked Varnadore to submit a plan to alleviate the odors and describe the contents of the solid waste.

Varnadore has 20 days to respond to the notice.

The Stuttgart Daily Leader, Wednesday, April 22, 1992

New York garbage shipped to DeWitt

LITTLE ROCK (AP) — Tons of New York garbage are in railroad cars in southeastern Arkansas, and the state says the odor is a public nuisance.

The state Department of Pollution Control and Ecology has issued a violation notice to D. Gray Varnadore, who operates a DeWitt landfill in which the solid waste is being dumped.

The waste is shipped from Brooklyn, N.Y.

Larry Wilson, PC&E deputy director, said Varnadore is storing hundreds of tons of solid waste in Stuttgart before taking it to the landfill.

The waste is being shipped by rail from New York to Southeast Arkansas Landfill Inc. Three or four box cars of solid waste arrive each week. The waste is kept in boxcars up to week before it is taken to DeWitt, Wilson said.

In the April 17 violation notice, PC&E asked Varnadore to submit a

(See DEWITT, page 2.)

DeWitt

(Continued from page one.)

plan to alleviate the odors and describe the contents of the solid waste.

"One of the concerns we have is we aren't sure what is being sent here," Wilson said. "In two inspections, we've seen no evidence of household hazardous waste, but we have seen some items that might have been medical waste."

Wilson said about 42 tons of waste are moved from the boxcars to the landfill each day. Under state law, a landfill cannot dispose of more than 50 tons of waste per day, he said.

PC&E learned about the waste storage when residents of a Stuttgart mobile home park complained about the odor, Wilson said.

Varnadore said Tuesday that he has a permit for disposing of out-of-state waste.

"We had off-loaded up there for over a month and there wasn't an odor problem until the trailer park residents found out the garbage was coming from out of state," Varnadore said.

In November 1991, the state obtained a temporary restraining order preventing a train from disposing of a 12,000-ton load of Maryland sewer sludge in Varnadore's landfill.

DEWITT BOUND – Trash from New York bound for a DeWitt landfill is unloaded in Stuttgart

N.Y. trash raises stink

By KEITH F. TALLEY
Staff Writer

Infectious medical waste wasn't found in an April 17 inspection of the solid waste being stored in railroad cars outside Stuttgart's city limits, according to Wendy Grandgeorge, an environment program specialist with the Arkansas Health Department.

"There were some rubber gloves and diapers found during the inspection, but those were probably used for home health care purposes," she said. "No infectious medical waste was found though."

"It looks like the state boys jumped the gun on that (medical waste)," said Gray Varnadore of DeWitt, owner of Arkansas Waste Services.

Arkansas Waste Services is the company that handles the hauling and offloading of the trash being stored on the railroad cars outside Stuttgart. The company then transports the waste to a DeWitt landfill owned by Southeast Arkansas Landfill Inc.

Much of the solid waste being stored on the boxcars are from Star Recycling out of Brooklyn, N.Y. The company removes the recyclable items from the trash before it sends the residuals to Arkansas Waste

Services, Varnadore said.

"We wouldn't have to bring in out-of-state garbage if we could get it from within the state," he said. "About 90 percent of the state's waste is handled by Waste Management in Pine Bluff. I would like to be able to handle more of the state's trash.

"Because of Waste Management's deep pockets and clout, it has been able to get most of the state's business. Even Arkansas County's trash is being handled by Waste Management."

Stuttgart's nasty stench

Most people think of Stuttgart as being synonymous with rice farming and wild ducks and, yes – we may as well go ahead and say it – lots of big mosquitoes. But not the stench of 150 tons of ripening refuse – including some, ugh, medical wastes – imported from Brooklyn, N.Y.

Responsible state officials should be ashamed for allowing Arkansas to become a dumping ground for solid wastes from some of the big cities of the East.

Three or four boxcars of odoriferous wastes are arriving weekly in Stuttgart and some are remaining sidetracked for up to a week before being unloaded and their putrid contents transported to a landfill near DeWitt.

No wonder local residents are up in arms and that Lt. Gov. Jim Guy Tucker is questioning contractor D. Gray Varnadore's operation. Tucker says he is concerned most of all because there hasn't been a public hearing on the issue.

Odd that public input has been excluded on such a sensitive issue as importing out-of-state wastes when our own state may someday need whatever landfills are available to dispose of our own wastes.

The fact that there hasn't been any public hearings raises an even larger issue. That is the question of who is in control of the situation at Stuttgart, the state Pollution Control and Ecology Department or Varnadore?

PC&E Director Larry Wilson says Varnadore was *required* to hold a public hearing and apply to PC&E for a permit *modification* before accepting any of these wastes. However, an article in Wednesday's *Democrat-Gazette* quotes Varnadore as saying that nothing in his PC&E permit requires him to hold a public hearing, that it in fact allows him to import Brooklyn's wastes.

Since he still hasn't allowed any public input and because of PC&E's past experience in dealing with him, Varnadore appears to be making the tail wag the dog – and getting away with it.

As for PC&E's past dealings with Varnadore, the agency's attorneys had to go to court last fall to stop him from bringing in a train – aptly dubbed the 'poopoo choo-choo" – loaded with, of all things, 12,000 tons of sewer sludge from Maryland.

Though PC&E sent Varnadore a violation notice last week concerning the Brooklyn wastes, the public hearing requirement apparently wasn't mentioned. Since he has a permit, was it modified by PC&E without benefit of the required public hearing, or is he operating despite the PC&E requirement?

The violation notice instructed Varnadore to submit a plan for alleviating the odors and to describe the contents of the imported wastes, but since he has 20 days to answer, public tempers may have cooled in the meantime.

Anyhow, Brooklyn's refuse is arriving faster than Varnadore's company can legally dispose of it at the rate of 42 tons a day. Is he in effect circumventing the state's 50-ton-a-day limit by storing boxcar loads of the wastes on rail cars at Stuttgart?

That's the most obvious reason we can think of for the stinky tie-up of refuse-laden boxcars sidetracked there. That situation should alert the Legislature to the need to bar any imports of out-of-state solid wastes to Arkansas.

"Hello," I said.

"Gray, this is Hattie Boone, and I am appalled by what you are trying to do, destroy this area by bring in Yankee money. This small southern community is known for working hard and making the south proud, raising rice and soybeans. Not bringing in Yankee money. I'll do everything possible to stop you from bringing this Yankee money to DeWitt. And I don't want it in my bank!" She slammed the phone down in my ear.

I turned around and looked at Amy. "That was the wildest phone call I have ever had." Then I retold the story to my wife.

To fully understand the conversation you need a little background on Miss. Hattie Boone Black. She was and eighty plus year old woman, one of the most wealthy persons in Arkansas County and owned the most farm land.

Miss Hattie and her sister owned the First National Bank so she pretty well ruled the roost in Arkansas County. She was a staunch southerner who had not been at all pleased that the South lost to the Yankees.

But Miss Hattie's ideals were skewed to fit her circumstances. She didn't want MY Yankee money put in her bank, but it didn't matter that she was selling her crops to the northerners "Yankee's" and putting their Yankee money in her bank. Hattie's complaints had nothing to do with the environmental impact of our landfill activity. She really had no environmental concerns.

Miss Hattie owned several co-ops and used to wait until there was a long weekend and then have all the co-ops waste tires burned on a Friday afternoon about sundown, not far from the landfill, on some ground she owned. Her whole rant had to do with money and control. She had the money and control. If she said black was white and next week said white was black it didn't matter the contradiction. She had a powerful control and had no intention of letting go.

I told Amy, we may not be in business much longer, between Clinton running for President and Hattie Boone, on the war path, the money and the politics may win out.

Later that morning after my little conversation with Hattie Boone, I went to the First National Bank to talk with the bank president Ray Hambrick. He was also a friend of our family; he and my dad were in the Navy and in World War II together.

I restated the story of Hattie's call to him. He burst out laughing, loud laughing and said that was the funniest thing he had heard in a while.

"Gray," he said, "her library in her house is full of books about how the northerners came down after the civil war and took advantage of the southern folk. When you leave the bank, walk out the west door, and walk across the street. Look at all her cars under the garage. You won't find one thing on those cars that says they were made in the north, but that's where she spent her money. She had all the tags and logos taken off before they were ever delivered."

And he was right. I went over and looked at the cars and there were no logos or any other identification clueing where the cars were made. Now the Mercedes! That was made in Germany, logos all over it, but not those Detroit, Yankee made cars.

I was ready for any environmental questions anybody had, because I knew the high quality of our facility and the fact I knew what I was doing. This wasn't rocket science! But to have to battle centuries old traditions that made no sense in the landfill business? I wasn't expecting those rules and regulations from an old southern belle.

*****

The Final Straw Days

Back to the Yankee garbage. My name was all over the news and it wasn't good news. The media was trying to paint me as a bad landfill operator. Attorney General, Winston Bryant saw his opportunity to get some badly needed media exposure. After Clinton put his hat in the ring for President, Attorney General Winston Bryant was bidding to be Governor. Winston filed a lawsuit seeking to close our landfill.

It seems this "Yankee Garbage" issue is not what brother Bill wants to deal with while running for the highest office in the land (Remember Clinton doesn't like for anyone to interrupt his day). Don't think it would look too good for the southern governor to allow "Yankee Garbage" to be dumped into his state. Every time Clinton flew back to town Winston was right there brown noise right up Clinton's ass on the tarmac, to brief him on the progress of the suit.

The April 23, 1992 article tells about the starting of the stink. "New York Trash Raises Stink." Very little odor actually came from Star Recycling waste sense Star Recycling had sprayed the waste with disinfectant and as you will read in the reports written by the ADPC&E they recorded very little odor. Continue on pg. **55.**

Civil lawsuit filed in trash dispute

DEWITT – Attorney General Winston Bryant filed a lawsuit today against an Arkansas County landfill operator for alleged violations of Arkansas laws regulating the storage, transportation, and handling of solid wastes.

"It is our intent to shutdown this operation until the Department of Pollution Control and Ecology has time to review the ability of the defendants to comply with Arkansas laws and regulations," Bryant said in a press conference held in DeWitt.

The civil suit, filed in Arkansas County Chancery Court, names Southeast Arkansas Landfill Inc. as a defendant.

According to the complaint filed by Attorney General Bryant, Southeast Arkansas Landfill is an Arkansas corporation which originally began operation of a non-hazardous landfill as Varnadore Sanitary Landfill at DeWitt in 1982. In 1988, the Varnadore family formed Southeast Arkansas Landfill to own and operate the landfill.

Southeast Arkansas Landfill filed Chapter 11 bankruptcy on Oct. 18, 1990 and closed in April of 1991. In December of 1991, the owners of Southeast Arkansas Landfill – John Carl Varnadore Sr., Mildred Varnadore, John Carl Varnadore Jr., and Douglas Gray Varnadore – entered into an agreement with Lester Pinkus of New York who purchased 20 percent ownership of the firm for $125,000.

Operations at the landfill resumed in early 1992 and on April 13, the Arkansas Department of Pollution Control and Ecology received complaints about odors from residents of a mobile home park located near the southern city limits of Stuttgart. According to an investigation by the PC&E, the source of the odors was boxcars of baled waste located on train tracks near the mobile home park.

The lawsuit alleges that Southeast Arkansas Landfill failed to inform the PC&E of a substantial increase in the volume of waste, failed to properly characterize its waste stream, and stores its wastes in a manner which constitutes a public nuisance or a public health hazard.

Additionally, Southeast Arkansas Landfill failed to notify the PC&E of Mr. Pinkus' purchase of a 20 percent ownership in the firm as required by PC&E regulations, according to the complaint.

Arkansas Democrat-Gazette/Scott Carpenter

OFFICIAL LOOK – Attorney General Winston Bryant (right) and Perrin Jones of the attorney general's staff view garbage packed into the back end of a boxcar in Stuttgart on Thursday.

Bryant sues to shut down landfill
Alleges violations at DeWitt dump taking N.Y. trash

BY JAKE SANDLIN
Democrat-Gazette Staff Writer

DEWITT – Citing "severe environmental problems," Attorney General Winston Bryant sued Thursday to temporarily, if not permanently, close Southeast Arkansas Landfill Inc. in Arkansas County.

"The information we have indicates that the landfill has potential problems that could cause irreparable harm to the groundwater in this area," Bryant said outside the Arkansas County Courthouse in DeWitt, where his representatives filed the lawsuit at 1 p.m.

Bryant said there would be a hearing on the suit Tuesday in chancery court at DeWitt. He said he would ask for an injunction to close the landfill just outside southeastern DeWitt.

Gray Varnadore of DeWitt, operator of the landfill, listened to the latter part of Bryant's news conference, then said his company would be ready with a defense by Tuesday.

"What it looks like to me is there's a lot of questions that they're trying to throw out to the public that they've already got the answers to if they just look in their own files," Varnadore said.

The out-of-state solid waste being taken to Varnadore's landfill drew publicity this week because it has been stored in railroad boxcars in

Garbage

• Continued from Page One

Stuttgart before being transferred by truck to the DeWitt landfill. Those transfers began in mid-March.

After a month, odor prompted residents of a mobile home park next to the tracks to call the state Department of Pollution Control & Ecology.

"I filed the lawsuit because there are severe environmental problems associated with the landfill," Bryant said. He added that he wants the injunction so the PC&E can address those problems, including analyzing the contents of the solid waste.

The landfill has been receiving solid waste from Star Recycling, a Brooklyn, N.Y., company that was recently fined $100,000 by environmental authorities in New York state, Bryant said. He did not elaborate on the violation for which that fine was assessed.

"We are concerned about the waste stream coming into the landfill and what the contents might be because of the past history of Star corporation," Bryant said. "We want a chance to look at the actual contents Star has coming into the landfill."

"Basically, the landfill operator is using the boxcars as a means of storing the solid waste" against PC&E instructions, Bryant said. "From our evidence, the waste is left in the boxcars, in many instances for up to one week before it is removed. You can imagine what would occur during the hot summertime if this practice continues."

Varnadore said the longest the boxcars sit with waste is "three days in one particular boxcar." He had identified his company that transfers the garbage from Stuttgart to the landfill as Arkansas Waste Services.

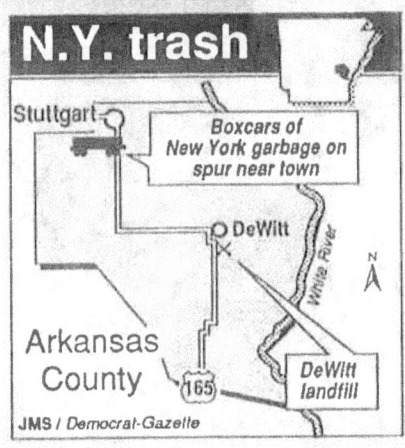

N.Y. trash

Stuttgart

Boxcars of New York garbage on spur near town

DeWitt

White River

Arkansas County

165

DeWitt landfill

N

JMS / Democrat-Gazette

Bryant listed as alleged violations:

• The amount of the imported solid waste is almost double what it was when the company's permit was re-issued in 1988, when only a 10 percent maximum increase is allowed. PC&E was not notified of any change.

• Southeast Arkansas Landfill and its operators have not brought the landfill up to Class 1 specifications, including the monitoring of the ground water as required by the PC&E. Linings and a collection system also must be installed.

• Possible medical waste is present in the solid waste.

• The company is storing solid waste in boxcars in Stuttgart to be under the maximum 50-ton daily limit on out-of-state solid waste accepted into the landfill.

• After Southeast Arkansas Landfill went into bankruptcy in October 1991, Lester Pinkus of New York contributed $125,000 in capital to the company for 20 percent ownership. This transfer of ownership and of the landfill permit is illegal, Bryant said, unless approved by the PC&E, which was not consulted.

• Star Recycling in New York has had "numerous problems with the environmental authorities in the state of New York," Bryant said, including the $100,000 fine. Bryant said Star began shipping the solid waste to Arkansas shortly after that fine was assessed.

Varnadore said the landfill area used so far isn't required to have a permit, but that upgrading of its engineering is in the works. He added that notifying the PC&E of any change in ownership of his company "is not a condition in my permit."

He also said he was not aware of any problems the Star company has had. "As a matter of fact, I have contacted (New York environmental officials) to ask their standing, and they told me that Star was in good shape."

Close the landfill

Attorney General Winston Bryant cited the best of all reasons — "severe environmental problems" — in filing for an injunction Thursday to close the Southeast Arkansas landfill where solid wastes from Brooklyn, N.Y., are being buried.

Based on information he has gathered, Bryant said — without elaborating — that potential problems at the landfill could do irreparable harm to the area's groundwater.

Whatever the dangers are, he will no doubt detail them during Tuesday's hearing on the injunction in chancery court at DeWitt. Among other things, state officials want to inspect the Brooklyn wastes to analyze its contents, which include medical wastes.

Landfill operator Gray Varnadore was in the crowd at Bryant's news conference Thursday on the steps of the Arkansas County Courthouse. His reaction was that Bryant had merely raised a strawman and that a lot of questions were thrown out to the public to which the state already had the answers.

Be that as it may, Bryant says Varnadore's landfill doesn't meet minimum standards and that he has neither monitored the ground water, as required by the Pollution Control and Ecology Department, nor installed certain safeguards.

Moreover, Bryant echoed our own concerns by accusing the company of circumventing the state's maximum 50-ton daily limit on out-of-state refuse by storing it in boxcars on a rail siding in Stuttgart. In addition, Bryant said Varnadore was importing almost double what his 1988 permit allows.

The attorney general also wants to pull the tie that binds Star Recycling — a Brooklyn company beset with numerous environmental problems — to Varnadore's company to see what unravels.

Star began its shipments of solid wastes to Arkansas shortly after state environmental authorities in New York fined Star $100,000. After Varnadore's firm filed for bankruptcy last fall, a New York man put $125,000 into the company for 20 percent ownership without the transfer of ownership and the landfill permit being submitted to PC&E as required by law.

Those are good and sufficent reasons for the court to grant at least a temporary injunction against the invasion of East Coast refuse in Arkansas.

Judge Russell Rogers is the one that issued an order to stop the offloading of the cars and that's when their world got stinky. If you stop the offloading process of rail cars and let the cars sit on the spur in 90 degree heat for 14 days, yeah, you have some stinky boxcars. That was not my company's fault that the town stinks like rotten garbage (read through the news articles and look at the cartoons that depict the propaganda about the offloading site as well as the landfill).

I'll never forget the morning of April 23, 1992 when the news reporter interviewed the lady in the trailer park talking about the smell how they just knew it was the material from NY City. She said it smell like sewage.

The real truth? Her sewer line had broken and was running freely under her house trailer, good reason why it smelled like sewage, but it was blamed on the spur and no one contested it at the time.

The manager of Thermogas, said they started smelling it on a warm day. The state came and sited Thermogas for washing chemicals down the ditch, but Judge Rogers didn't shut their business down. It was only the out of state situation from New York that was charged with environmental damage and closed down. Local dumping didn't count against the environmental issues I guess.

Even though Judge Rogers was aware of the positive report from the ADPC&E inspectors (read over their reports and see what they have to say), he still ruled to close the landfill.

I remember the Friday afternoon the Deputy Director of ADPC&E, Larry Wilson, called my home wanting to speak to the enforcement head, Harry Elliot. I took Harry to my home so he could call his boss, from my phone.

Larry wanted to know if the agency had found anything at all they could use to shut us down. Harry told him no, not from the out-of-state waste but, the local garbage that comes from the City of DeWitt might be a different story. Larry told him to keep looking. The state had conducted their inspection and found nothing. That's right nothing, but that wasn't the issue. It wasn't about the quality of the waste or the operation. It was where the waste was comimg from "New York City" and Clinton running for President. The whole issue was about politics.

After the state had conducted all of their inspections at the site and offloading facility and found no problems I received a call from my lawyer. Continue on pg. **82.**

Around Arkansas

Arkansas Democrat-Gazette/Scott Carpenter

A STINK IN ARKANSAS COUNTY — Attorney General Winston Bryant views garbage packed into the back end of a boxcar in Stuttgart on Thursday.

CITING "SEVERE ENVIRONMENTAL problems," Attorney General Winston Bryant sued Thursday to temporarily, if not permanently, close Southeast Arkansas Landfill Inc. in Arkansas County. The importation of the out-of-state garbage has been raising a stink, state officials said last Tuesday.

Larry Wilson, deputy director of the state Department of Pollution Control and Ecology, said the owner of a landfill apparently is creating an odor nuisance by storing hundreds of tons of solid waste in Stuttgart before taking it to a DeWitt landfill. The waste is shipped from Brooklyn, N.Y.

There will be a hearing on Bryant's suit Tuesday in DeWitt.

The waste is being shipped by rail from New York to Southeast Arkansas Landfill Inc. Three or four boxcars of solid waste arrive each week. The waste is kept in boxcars as long as a week before it is taken to DeWitt, Wilson said.

D. Gray Varnadore, who operates the landfill, said Tuesday he has a permit for disposing out-of-state waste.

Our Opinion

Trashing Stuttgart

The city of Stuttgart begins its annual Cleanup Week today, but the event, sponsored by the Stuttgart Chamber of Commerce, begins on a sour note. Stuttgart has been deluged with bad statewide publicity this past week thanks to a DeWitt family who owns and operates a landfill in south Arkansas County.

The city received plenty of statewide publicity last week after it was learned that the DeWitt company the family owns was shipping garbage from New York through Stuttgart.

The company, Southeast Arkansas Landfill Inc., was unloading the garbage – shipped in boxcars from Brooklyn, N.Y. – at a location just outside the city limits on the south end of town. The garbage was unloaded from the boxcars onto trucks and transported to a landfill in DeWitt.

Attorney General Winston Bryant paid our fair city a visit last week to file a lawsuit seeking to stop Southeast Arkansas Landfill Inc., from bringing any more New York garbage into Arkansas County.

First, a little background is required. Southeast Arkansas Landfill began operation in 1982 as Varnadore Sanitary Landfill. Southeast Arkansas Landfill was originally owned by the Varnadore family of DeWitt, but the company filed for bankruptcy in 1990.

In December 1991, the owners of Southeast Arkansas Landfill – John Carl Varnadore Sr., Mildred Varnadore, John Carl Varnadore Jr., and Douglas Gray Varnadore – entered into an agreement with Lester Pinkus of Dermott, who purchased 20 percent ownership of the firm for $125,000, according to the attorney general's office.

Before long the company was shipping garbage from New York into Arkansas County. Gray Varnadore says the lawsuit filed by Mr. Bryant is politics, pure and simple, and that he and his family are operating within the limits of the law.

But serious questions remain, according to Mr. Bryant. Questions we're glad to see Mr. Bryant raising, regardless of his motives.

Mr. Bryant says the Varnadores' landfill doesn't meet minimum standards and that Southeast Arkansas Landfill Inc. failed to monitor the ground water as required by the Pollution Control and Ecology Department.

But the most serious charge raised against the Varnadores is the one concerning the amount of out of state garbage being shipped to the landfill in DeWitt.

Mr. Bryant has accused the company of circumventing the state's maximum 50-ton daily limit on out of state refuse by storing the refuse in boxcars just outside the city limits of Stuttgart.

Mr. Bryant says the Varnadore family is importing almost double what their 1988 permit allows. If this allegation proves to be true, then Mr. Bryant's probe is on the right track, and the Varnadores' garbage is on the wrong tracks, notably those outside the city limits of Stuttgart.

We'll find out Tuesday who is right. A chancery court hearing is set for Tuesday in DeWitt and a judge will rule whether the Varnadore family can continue shipping New York garbage into Arkansas County.

You can be sure the statewide media will be there and more bad publicity for Arkansas County will be sure to follow thanks to the Varnadores.

ARKANSAS DEPARTMENT OF POLLUTION CONTROL AND ECOLOGY

MEMORANDUM

TO   : Suzanne Stair, Inspector Supervisor

FROM   : Keith Helm, Inspector

DATE   : April 27, 1992

SUBJECT : Southeast Arkansas Landfill

===

Railcar off loading Spur

Steve Henderson, Air Inspector and I inspected this site on Monday, April 13, 1992. The site is located adjacent to the southern city limits of Stuttgart. A complaint of odor problems had been transmitted to me from a resident of a nearby mobile home park late Friday afternoon, April the 10th.

Three to four railcars of bailed waste are spurred off here each week since early March.

The waste is kept locked in the railcars until it is off loaded through a covered dock to a covered trailer truck that transport the bailed waste to the SEA Landfill located northeast of DeWitt.

As we observed the off/on loading operation, I noticed some odor within 15-30 feet of the site. Photos were taken.

At this point in time we decided the Solid Waste Division should continue with the investigation. I returned Steve to the office, I returned to the site, and waited for a loaded trailer truck then follow the truck to SEA Landfill.

Landfill site and operation

Upon arriving at the landfill I discussed the operations with the operators and Gray Varnadore. I performed an ADPC&E landfill inspection and evaluation.

The general appearance, work force, and equipment on site appeared greatly improved over past I&E's.

The waste stream is questionable. It appears to be solid waste that has had recyclables picked out (metal/cans, newsprint/paper, plastic containers, etc.).

I did not note anything I define specific as infectious waste; however, I did see medical tubing, feeder bags, rubber gloves, large diapers (bed pads).

A small amount of used tires are in the waste stream. Mr. Varnadore is sending those back on the returning railcars. The tires continuing to show makes me question the control at the generating site of the remainder of the waste stream. Photos were taken.

kh-graymemo

ARKANSAS DEPARTMENT OF POLLUTION CONTROL AND ECOLOGY

MEMORANDUM

TO   : Tom Boston, Chief, Solid Waste Division

THROUGH   : Joe Doughty, Engineer Supervisor

FROM   : Rodger Payne, Engineer

DATE   : 19-May-1992

SUBJECT   : Southeast Arkansas Landfill   Permit No. 198-S
             Offloading and Disposal   CSN 01-0117
             of Baled Recycle Waste

On Monday, May 18, 1992, Suzanne Stair and the writer travelled to Stuttgart and DeWitt to observe disposal of baled recycle waste at the referenced landfill as requested. It was warm (80s) and mostly sunny in the morning with late afternoon cloudiness and rain.

We met Keith Helm at the railroad siding at Stuttgart to observe the day's first offloading of bales. At about 7:20 a.m., a fork lift driver and bobcat driver arrived at the site and began preparing to offload bales. Offloading began at about 7:40 a.m., primarily with the fork lift. Bales were removed from the boxcar, parked at a offloading platform, to an adjacent trailer truck. To facilitate unloading of the trailer later @ the landfill, a cable was wrapped around the bales from the front of the trailer all the way to the back end during loading operations. Loading of the first trailer was completed at about 8:00 a.m. There was only one trailer available for transport this date. A second trailer (which had been used on Friday, 5-15-92) was down because of burnt-out bearings.

During loading, Suzanne Stair, Keith Helm and the writer walked around the boxcars at the siding; no liquid was observed draining from the boxcars. Also, no odor was detected beyond the immediate vicinity of the off-loading operation.

After loading of the first trailer was completed, Suzanne Stair, Keith Helm and the writer travelled to the referenced landfill, a distance of approximately 32 miles. The first trailer load arrived at the landfill at about 9:00 a.m. It took only about five minutes to unload the trailer - a dozer simply pulled the bales out with the cable (mentioned in the second paragraph above). Once the bales had been unloaded, retaining wires of each bale were cut and contents spread about with a dozer and compactor. The contents of bales were observed with particular emphasis on finding any waste of a infectious or suspicious nature (not typically domestic or commercial). A few I.V. bags and tubes were noticed (none with needles or fluid). The waste was a mixture typical of household and commercial waste streams with no unusual contents. Following observation of disposal of the first load of baled waste, ADPC&E personnel returned to the siding at Stuttgart.

Personnel and equipment on-hand at the landfill this date included:

Personnel	Equipment
- Johnny Varnadore, Supervisor	- CAT 816 steel wheeled compactor w/front blade
- Compactor operator	- CAT D6C dozer
- Dozer operator/scraper operator	- John Deere 4960 tractor w/Cameco earth scraper

Gray Varnadore came on-site two or three times in the afternoon to observe and discuss operations with operating personnel and Department representatives.

Loading of the second trailer load was completed at 10:40 a.m. Keith Helm remained at the siding to observe subsequent loading operations. Suzanne Stair and the writer returned to the landfill to observe unloading operations. The second trailer load arrived at the landfill at 11:30 a.m. A third trailer load arrived at the landfill at 2:30 p.m. The contents of the second and third loads of baled waste were inspected and nothing unusual was found.

The writer measured a total of five bales in order to estimate the average volume of a bale. It should be emphasized that due to the very irregular edges of the bales, it was difficult to get exact, representative measurements. Based upon measurements, the average volume of a bale disposed of on May 18 is estimated to be approximately 2.6 cubic yards.

No facilities were available for weighing bales. However, based upon a conversation with Lester Pillow of the Northeast Arkansas Solid Waste Disposal Authority (a facility which uses a solid waste disposal baling system), it is estimated that the baled density of waste disposed of was roughly 1200 pounds/cubic yard or 3,100 $\pm$ pounds per bale. Field measurements and calculations of the average volume of a bale are shown on Page 3.

Around 4:30 p.m., it began a steady rain at the landfill. A fourth trailer load of baled waste arrived at the landfill at about 4:50 p.m. Due to the rain which caused the incline up to the fill area to become slippery, Gray Varnadore decided to leave the trailer parked on-site overnight and unload it around 7 - 7:30 a.m. the next morning (Wednesday). Suzanne Stair and the writer left the landfill about 5:10 p.m. and travelled to Stuttgart where we left word with Keith Helm to be on-hand at the landfill Wednesday to observe unloading.

ARKANSAS DEPARTMENT OF POLLUTION CONTROL AND ECOLOGY

MEMORANDUM

TO: File

FROM: Suzanne Stair, Inspector Supervisor, SWD

DATE: 27-APR-92

SUBJECT: AWS and SEAL Investigation

On April 21, 1992, Heidi Love, Inspector, SWD, and I performed an investigation of Arkansas Waste Services and Southeast Arkansas Landfill at the request of Larry Wilson, Deputy Director. We arrived at 11:30 hours in Stuttgart at the railroad spur of AWS. This spur is for the off-loading from boxcars of waste from Star Recycling. Employees of AWS said it takes about five truckloads to empty one boxcar full of baled waste. Still photographs and a video were taken of the spur, building for off-loading, some off-loading and the surrounding area. Rail cars are set when AWS calls for them, ie., when AWS unloads a car the railroad will pull it out and set another full one by the building to be off-loaded. While we were onsite AWS finished off-loading one car and there were two full cars to be off-loaded plus another full car was set by the railroad at 11:45 AM. Very little odor was detected and that was only within 15-20 feet of the building and the railcar being off-loaded. It should be noted that it was very windy all day at both locations. We left the AWS site at 12:00 hours.

We then went to DeWitt SEAL location and arrived at 13:15 hours. Mr. Johnny Varnadore was onsite with two other employees. The trailer that we observed being off-loaded arrived at approximately 14:00 hours. The trailer was unloaded, the baling was cut and the bales were spread and compacted immediately. Still photographs and videos were taken of these actions. Tires were pulled out of the waste and put back onto the trailer. These are sent back to Star in the empty boxcars. We did not see any waste that looked like medical waste as Keith Helm had observed on his April 13, 1992. We did not observe any glass, aluminum cars (although bimetal cars were observed), cardboard (except some cardboard still nailed to boards), plastic liter soft drink or milk carton bottles, or white office paper. We did observe a small amount of yard waste, paper that is not recycled (telephone books and catalogues), a few tires (these are pulled and sent back to Star), plastic bags, florist foam, and cloth and material.

Mr. Gray Varnadore arrived onsite during the compacting of the waste. He asked both of us about the appearance of the landfill in comparison to the inspection of August, 1990. We both agreed that the landfill had improved greatly. This is probably due to the fact that there were more employees and equipment on site than in previous inspections. We left the site at 15:30 hours.

Arkansas Democrat 🦅 Gazette
● ● WEDNESDAY, APRIL 29, 1992

Judge prohibits garbage transfers at Stuttgart tracks

BY ANDY GOTLIEB
Democrat-Gazette State Desk

A circuit-chancery judge issued a temporary restraining order Tuesday prohibiting Southeast Arkansas Landfill Inc. from unloading or storing garbage at a Stuttgart site.

Also Tuesday, a hearing on Attorney General Winston Bryant's lawsuit seeking to close a DeWitt landfill operated by the firm was postponed until May 5.

The restraining order was issued by Circuit-Chancery Judge Russell Rogers of Stuttgart.

"This is great news," Bryant said. "We're very pleased."

Landfill operator Gray Varnadore of DeWitt (Arkansas County) could not be reached for comment Tuesday afternoon. But Varnadore's brother, Johnny Varnadore, said he had not heard about the order.

"It's going to cost us a pretty good sum of money," he said.

Citing "severe environmental problems," Bryant sued last Thursday to temporarily – if not permanently – close the landfill. He said the landfill's continued operation could cause irreparable harm to area ground water.

Out-of-state solid wastes being taken to the landfill drew publicity last week because the wastes were stored in railroad boxcars in Stuttgart. The wastes were then transferred by truck to the DeWitt landfill.

Those transfers, conducted by a subsidiary of Southeast Arkansas Landfill, began in mid-March.

After a month, odor prompted residents of a mobile home park next to the Stuttgart railroad tracks to call the state Department of Pollution Control and Ecology.

The order by Rogers prohibits Southeast Arkansas Landfill from "storing or unloading any garbage or other waste, whether located in railroad boxcars, box-type trailers designed to be pulled by trucks, or in any other form or manner, at the railroad siding ... (in) Stuttgart."

Rogers wrote that it "appears the chances of success of the plaintiff upon the merits of its allegations are significant."

The order does not prohibit the landfill from continuing operations.

"That will be one of the many things we'll be asking for next week," Bryant said. "Our complaint goes into the entire process."

Layoff notices come for 4 workers in trash dispute

By KEITH F. TALLEY
Staff Writer

The temporary restraining order issued Tuesday prohibiting the storing and unloading of trash from a waste storage site located near the southern city limits of Stuttgart has resulted in the layoff of four people, according to Johnny Varnadore, an owner of Southeast Arkansas Landfill Inc.

"We had to layoff four people yesterday afternoon," Varnadore said. "Three people from Arkansas Waste Services and one from the landfill had to be let go."

The restraining order, filed by Prosecuting Attorney Robert Dittrich of Stuttgart, was issued because residents near the storage site continued complaining about the odor coming from trash-laden boxcars.

The trash is stored at the site before it is taken to a DeWitt landfill owned by members of the Varnadore family.

"I have no comment on how bad the odor is going to get over there now that we can't offload the trash," Varnadore said.

"My personal opinion on the matter is that it's political."

(See LAYOFF, page 2.)

Layoff

(Continued from page one.)

Varnadore said according to an article in the *Arkansas Democrat-Gazette*, Hillary Clinton, wife of Gov. Bill Clinton, sits on the board of directors of a hazardous waste company located in Arkansas.

"If we could afford to pay Hillary Clinton $30,000 a year to be on our board of directors," he said, "we probably wouldn't be getting all of this harassment."

The restraining order is part of a civil lawsuit filed by Dittrich in the Northern District of Arkansas County Chancery Court.

A hearing on this lawsuit and another civil lawsuit filed by Attorney General Winston Bryant against the DeWitt landfill will be reviewed in Arkansas County Chancery Court at 1 p.m. May 5 in DeWitt.

Attorney General Bryant Files Suit Against DeWitt Landfill Operator

Attorney General Winston Bryant filed a lawsuit April 23 against an Arkansas County landfill operator for alleged violations of Arkansas laws regulating the storage, transportation, and handling of solid wastes.

"It is our intent to shutdown this operation until the Department of Pollution Control and Ecology has time to review the ability of the defendants to comply with Arkansas laws and regulations," Attorney General Bryant said in a press conference held in DeWitt.

The civil suit, filed in Arkansas County Chancery Court, names Southeast Arkansas Landfill, Inc. as a defendant.

According to the complaint filed by Attorney General Bryant, Southeast Arkansas Landfill is an Arkansas corporation which originally began operation of a nonhazardous landfill as Varnadore Sanitary Landfill at DeWitt in 1982. In 1986, the Varnadore family formed Southeast Arkansas Landfill to own and operate the landfill.

Southeast Arkansas Landfill filed Chapter 11 bankruptcy on Oct. 18, 1990 and closed in April of 1991. In December of 1991, the owners of Southeast Arkansas Landfill — John Carl Varndore, Sr., Mildred Varnadore, John Carl Varnadore, Jr., and Douglas Gray Varndore — entered into an agreement with Lester Pinkus of New York who purchased 20% ownership

of the firm for $125,000.

Operations at the landfill resumed in early 1992 and on April 13, the Arkansas Department of Pollution Control and Ecology received complaints about odors from residents of a mobile home park located near the southern city limits of Stuttgart. According to an investigation by the ADPC&E, the source of the odors was boxcars of baled waste located on train tracks near the mobile home park.

The lawsuit alleges that Southeast Arkansas Landfill failed to inform the ADPC&E of a substantial increase in the volume of waste, failed to properly characterize its waste stream, and stores its wastes in a manner which constitutes a public nuisance or a public health hazard.

Additionally, Southeast Arkansas Landfill failed to notify the ADPC&E of Mr. Pinkus' purchase of a 20% ownership in the firm as required by ADPC&E regulation, according to the complaint.

The suit asks for an order enjoining Southeast Arkansas Landfill from operating and requests a hearing at the court's earliest possible date.

A circuit-chancery judge issued a temporary restraining order Tuesday prohibiting Southeast Arkansas Landfill Inc. from unloading or storing garbage at a Stuttgart site.

Also Tuesday a hearing on Attorney

Winston Bryant
Attorney General

General Winston Bryant's lawsuit seeking to close a DeWitt landfill operated by the firm was postponed until May 5.

The restraining order was issued by Circuit-Chancery Judge Russell Rogers of Stuttgart.

Winston Bryant, a native of Donaldson (Hot Spring County), Arkansas, was elected Attorney General in November of 1990. As Attorney General, he is the attorney for state officials, agencies, boards, and commissions. The Attorney General is also responsible for providing legal opinions with regard to the state's criminal and civil laws.

Attorney General Bryant has previously served the state of Arkansas as Lieutenant Governor, Secretary of State, and State Representative. He is past chairman of the National Conference of Lieutenant Governors and is founder and chairman of the Arkansas Youth Suicide Prevention Commission.

Mr. Bryant is a Cum Laude graduate of Ouachita Baptist University. He later received a law degree from the University of Arkansas and went on to obtain his Masters of Law from George Washington University in Washington, D.C. Following college, Mr. Bryant entered the United States Army and earned the rank of Captain.

In addition to public service, Winston Bryant has had extensive legal and legislative experience since becoming licensed to practice law in 1963. He worked as a legislative assistant to the late Senator John L. McClellan and has served as an attorney for the Arkansas Insurance Commission. He was also a deputy prosecuting attorney for the Arkansas Insurance Commission. He was also a deputy prosecuting attorney, as well as assistant United States Attorney for the Eastern District of Arkansas.

Winston Bryant served four terms as Arkansas' Lieutenant Governor and is considered by many to have been the most active Lieutenant Governor in the state's history. He assumed the duties of Attorney General on January 15, 1991, and has restructured the office to become more active in consumer affairs, utility regulation, fighting child abuse, and addressing the needs of elderly Arkansans.

NYC waste at landfill topic of DeWitt hearing

BY JOE FARMER
Democrat-Gazette Pine Bluff Bureau

DeWITT — An investor in a Stuttgart landfill being sued to stop operation is from Dermott, not New York.

That was one of the facts that came out as the owners of Southeast Arkansas Landfill were in Arkansas County Chancery Court here Tuesday afternoon. They were answering a lawsuit filed by Attorney General Winston Bryant after several boxcar loads of New York City waste were found on a Stuttgart railroad siding near the dump site.

Bryant said the state still is under a moratorium blocking out-of-state waste until the Legislature can adopt a plan to control its flow.

The lawsuit asking for the tests is a way of enforcing that ban, Bryant said.

The hearing opened at 2 p.m. Tuesday. It is expected to continue this afternoon and Thursday, Bryant said, before Circuit-Chancery Judge Russell Rogers of Stuttgart.

However, defense attorney Charles S. Gibson Sr. of Dermott said the lawsuit is aimed at closing the dump, operated by Gary Varnadore.

Gibson said published reports that the site was saved from bankruptcy by a $125,000 investment from New York were wrong.

Gibson said published reports that the site was saved from bankruptcy by a $125,000 investment from New York were wrong.

In fact, he said, the money came from Lester Pinkus of Dermott (Chicot County) and would barely pay the cost of the tests being sought.

The state's key witness Tuesday afternoon was Larry Wilson, a deputy director of the state Department of Pollution Control and Ecology. He oversees its solid waste division.

Wilson testified that the company had a history of problems dating back to its receiving a permit in 1981. Most recently, he said, it was declared bankrupt in 1991, but continued to operate.

He said the operation was at a good site, but was underfunded.

"This is an excellent site if it can be brought up to standards and operate as a Class 1 landfill," Wilson testified. That is the state's highest landfill rating.

On cross-examination, Gibson showed several letters from the department saying the five-acre site was a Class 1 site.

"Those were written during a period of transition," Wilson said. "We were very lenient with them. We wanted them to operate."

Gibson said someone told the news media that the investor was from New York, when he is from Dermott. Also, Gibson said, someone said the company was fined $100,000 for improperly disposing of hazardous wastes.

The hearing is to resume at 1 p.m. today.

Stuttgart Daily Leader

Rice and Duck Capitol of the World — May 12, 1992

Testimony ends in local trash hearing

By KEITH F. TALLEY
Staff Writer

Testimony concerning civil lawsuits filed in Arkansas County Chancery Court against a DeWitt landfill and a waste storage site near Stuttgart ended yesterday.

Circuit-Chancery Judge Russell Rogers of Stuttgart told the attorneys for the defense and the state to send him letter briefs instead of going through lengthy closing arguments. He wants the briefs by May 18 so that he can make a ruling on the lawsuits.

When testimony ended, Rogers first decided to allow five boxcars loaded with trash at the site near Stuttgart to be emptied.

"I think more damage would be done just letting it sit there at the site than to bring it on into the landfill," Rogers said. "The worst scenario, I think, would be leaving it there."

Defense attorney Charles S. Gibson of Dermott then notified the court four more trash-laden boxcars were sitting somewhere on the railroad line in Stuttgart. He wanted those boxcars to be emptied too.

Attorney General Winston Bryant and Prosecuting Attorney Robert Dittrich of Stuttgart objected to this request.

"I think the best solution would be to send the boxcars back to their point of origin," Bryant said.

Dittrich pointed out that the controversy began with three boxcars of trash, and now nine boxcars of trash are involved.

Rogers told the attorneys to work out an agreement among themselves about what to do with the nine boxcars. He told the attorneys he would be in Lonoke today if any questions should arise.

"No decisions have been made as of this morning," Dittrich said. "The involved attorneys and the PC&E (Arkansas Department of Pollution Control and Ecology) are still trying to work out a suitable arrangement."

He also said bringing more boxcars to the site was technically a violation of the temporary restraining order that was signed April 28 by Rogers.

The controversy began in late March when residents of a mobile home park began complaining about an odor coming from boxcars sitting on a nearby railroad spur.

(see TRASH page 8A.)

69

Trash

(continued from page one.)

The railroad spur, located near the soutem city limits of Stuttgart, was being used as a storage site before the trash was offloaded to a DeWitt landfill owned by Southeast Arkansas Landfill Inc.

It was later established the trash, which is baled municipal waste, was coming from Star Recycling Inc. out of Brooklyn, N.Y.

The attorney general became concerned about what was in the baled waste and filed a civil lawsuit April 23 against the DeWitt landfill. The lawsuit alleged the landfill violated Arkansas laws regulating the storage, transportation and handling of solid wastes.

Dittrich filed a lawsuit April 28 against Gray Varnadore and the companies involved with the waste storage site in Stuttgart. The restraining order that was issued against the storage site resulted from the April 28 lawsuit.

Gray Varnadore is an owner of the DeWitt landfill and of Arkansas Waste Services, which operates the storage site near Stuttgart.

Gibson has maintained throughout the hearing the only reason the state filed lawsuits against the DeWitt landfill and the waste storage site was because the landfill was accepting trash from out of state.

A.H. Ludwig, a geologist and witness for the defense, testified yesterday the DeWitt landfill was located in an ideal location since the groundwater was beneath a 58-foot layer of clay.

The state contended, however, the groundwater underneath the site could be contaminated since iron and other heavy metals were detected in a February water quality test at the landfill.

"I don't see any evidence," Ludwig said, "of ground water contamination at the DeWitt landfill."

Gibson also entered into evidence a memo from Tony Morris, a geologist at PC&E, stating the Shannon Road Landfill contained some of the highest sulfate, chloride and TDS (total dissolved solids) values in the state.

The Shannon Road Landfill is owned by Waste Management out of Pine Bluff and accepts waste from Arkansas County, Gibson said.

Arkansas Democrat 🐎 Gazette
• • WEDNESDAY MAY 13, 1992

Fate of odorous boxcars up in air

BY JOE FARMER
Democrat-Gazette Pine Bluff Bureau

STUTTGART – The sides in a lawsuit that wants boxcars of New York solid waste moved from this Arkansas County town couldn't reach an agreement Tuesday on what to do with them.

Circuit-Chancery Judge Russell Rogers of Stuttgart, who heard testimony over four days in Arkansas County Chancery Court at DeWitt on dual lawsuits on the matter, was to rule on the issue of what to do with the boxcars Tuesday, but he was in a trial at Lonoke (Lonoke County) and hadn't announced a decision.

In the final day of hearings Monday afternoon at DeWitt, defense attorney Charles S. Gibson of Dermott (Chicot County) said there were five cars on a rail spur owned by SouthEast Arkansas Landfill Inc. and four more on a Southern Pacific Railroad spur, all at Stuttgart.

Tuesday afternoon, Gibson said in one case there actually are only three cars on the railroad spur, or a total of eight. The misinformation came from the railroad, he said.

"The judge is on record twice as saying they could dispose of the five cars on their spur, and we are going to stick with that position," Gibson said. "We also feel the other three should be taken to the landfill. There was absolutely no evidence of any physical damage or harm to anyone."

A series of lawsuits was filed by state Attorney General Winston Bryant and Prosecuting Attorney Robert Dittrich of Stuttgart after neighbors com-

See GARBAGE, Page 3B

Garbage

• Continued from Arkansas Page

plained about the odor from three original boxcars of waste. Bryant, who attended the entire hearing, is representing the state Department of Pollution Control and Ecology.

Rogers issued a restraining order April 28 stopping the company from using the Stuttgart off-loading dock it owns. The landfill is near DeWitt.

Gray Varnadore, majority owner of the company, said at the time that another boxcar or two might be en route from Star Recycling Inc. of Brooklyn, N.Y., which originates the baled waste shipments.

Bryant said in a typed statement that his office wants the boxcars returned.

"The state contends that all boxcars should be returned to the generator," Bryant said. "Although the court expressed some concern about shipping the waste back to the generator, the state believes that returning the waste poses no greater risk to human health than offloading the waste onto trucks and transporting it to the SEAL landfill. Of course, if the court does not accept the state's position, then the state requests that it be given notice and opportunity to monitor the offloading of the boxcars."

Rogers combined the lawsuits, which seek a number of things, mainly to keep the Stuttgart loading dock closed and to close the landfill for more water tests by PC&E. Department officials testified that would cost about $125,000 and take 30 to 60 days.

Varnadore testified that he and his family operated the landfill until it went bankrupt last year. He now owns 80 percent of Arkansas Waste Systems Inc., which hauls the waste, and the new SouthEast Arkansas landfill.

He said he sold 20 percent of the companies to Lester Pinkus of Dermott for $125,000 and has about $15,000 left after making overdue debts current and buying new equipment and trucks.

However, he said, he could raise enough money to pay for the water tests, though he doesn't think they'll cost as much as the state estimates.

The company gets $580 for the hauling company and $520 for the landfill for each boxcar it processes, he said. It has 11 employees and must pay an $80-a-day penalty to the railroad after it has held the cars more than 48 hours.

"They are paying that on the five boxcars right now," Gibson said. "I don't think it has started on the other three, yet."

Rogers told the attorneys Monday afternoon that he wanted written closing arguments by next Monday and would rule on the lawsuits by the middle of the week.

However, department inspectors checked four leaking boxcars of the five on the company spur last weekend and took a sample from one.

Bryant said in his Tuesday response that it would take two to three weeks for the department to analyze that sample.

"Mr. Gray Varnadore's testimony revealed that the company's financial resources are severely limited," Bryant said in the response. "Should closure or remediation of the site become necessary, the funds would not be available from SEAL, and the burden of providing those funds could be shifted to the citizens of Arkansas."

Arkansas Democrat Gazette
● ● THURSDAY, MAY 14, 1992

Bury dripping N.Y. trash quickly, judge says

BY ANDY GOTLIEB
Democrat-Gazette State Desk

STUTTGART – New York garbage packing eight leaky railroad cars should be buried in an Arkansas landfill with "all due haste," Circuit-Chancery Judge Russell Rogers of Stuttgart ordered Wednesday.

The boxcars are to be unloaded and the garbage taken to the SouthEast Arkansas Landfill Inc. at DeWitt (Arkansas County), Rogers ordered. Any cars not unloaded by noon Tuesday will be shipped back to Star Recycling Inc. of Brooklyn, N.Y., he stated.

In a letter to the parties involved, Rogers explained why he chose to allow the garbage be buried instead of ordering it shipped back to New York, as Attorney General Winston Bryant had asked.

Rogers said he would rule on the lawsuit to close the landfill next week.

"The potential for harm from the garbage is greater sitting on a spur in Stuttgart or traveling several states on the railroad, oozing along the way, than is burying it in even a non-complying landfill," Rogers wrote. "Greed, coupled with the snail's pace of government, leaves the public at risk."

Much of the waste has been sitting on the railroad spur since April 28, when Rogers issued a restraining order blocking the unloading of the boxcars until suits regarding the disputed landfill are settled.

Bryant is trying to close the DeWitt landfill, alleging that it doesn't comply with state regulations. The suit was combined with a similar one filed by Prosecuting Attorney Robert Dittrich of Stuttgart.

Bryant filed his suit after residents of a mobile home park near the spur complained of odors from the boxcars, but the odors worsened after the restraining order was issued.

A state Pollution Control and Ecology Department inspector reported last week that the boxcars were beginning to ooze an unknown liquid.

On Tuesday, Charles S. Gibson of Dermott (Chicot County) – who represents landfill majority owner Gray Varnadore – asked Rogers to let the garbage be buried at the landfill. Bryant said the state should be allowed to test the liquid before the garbage was buried. He said it would take three to six weeks to test, a fact Rogers criticized.

"It is simply inconceivable to me that it should take three to six weeks to analyze the liquid oozing from the cars," he wrote. "If the State cannot expedite the tests, a private lab should be used."

Rogers did set three conditions related to the garbage. They are:

● PC&E shall have employees present when the garbage is unloaded and also go to the landfill to "inspect, test, observe and advise." If there is any cause for alarm, the process should stop and the court should be notified.

● The state should expedite the trash disposal.

● One-third of any revenues received by the landfill from the eight boxcars shall be set aside in a reserve account to

See GARBAGE, Page 5B

Garbage

● Continued from Arkansas Page

defray any resulting cleanup costs.

Both Bryant and Gibson expressed mixed opinions about the ruling.

"My position is that the waste should have been returned to the point of origin; however, I can understand the judge's ruling," he said in a statement. "This is at least a partial victory for us because it means that no more boxcars of waste will be shipped into this landfill until this matter is settled in court."

Bryant said the state would not appeal because it would be time-consuming and add to the existing problems in Stuttgart.

Gibson said the delays already have hurt his client. He said Varnadore's work force has disappeared.

"The wherewithal to deal with it in a timely fashion is questionable at this time," Gibson said, noting that Varnadore's business with the New York firm also has suffered.

Gibson said the state was overreacting to the ooze dripping from the boxcars. He described it an non-hazardous "garbage-type moisture."

"PC&E knows this, but they're having to run to the tune of the attorney general," he said.

Arkansas Democrat-Gazette/Steve Scallion

Arkansas Democrat-Gazette/Mike Stewart

CUTTING THE BALES – Steve London cuts the wire wrapping garbage bales at the SouthEast Arkansas Landfill near DeWitt (Arkansas County). The controversial garbage from New York prompted Attorney General Winston Bryant to file a lawsuit seeking to close the landfill.

Boxcars of garbage finally at landfill

BY ANDY GOTLIEB
Democrat-Gazette State Desk

STUTTGART – Workers on Friday began unloading the boxcars loaded with New York garbage that have sat on a railroad spur since late April.

The garbage was transported to DeWitt (Arkansas County) to be buried at the nearby SouthEast Arkansas Landfill Inc. Most of one of the seven boxcars was unloaded by Friday afternoon, Keith Helm, an inspector with the state Department of Pollution Control and Ecology, said. Helm was overseeing the unloading.

The garbage was transported to DeWitt (Arkansas County) to be buried at the nearby SouthEast Arkansas Landfill Inc. Most of one of the seven boxcars was unloaded by Friday afternoon, Keith Helm, an inspector with the state Department of Pollution Control and Ecology, said. Helm was overseeing the unloading.

"It seems like it's going pretty smooth," Helm said.

Circuit-Chancery Judge Russell Rogers of Stuttgart ordered Wednesday that the garbage be buried with "all due haste." He said any wastes not buried by noon Tuesday must be shipped back to Star Recycling Inc. of Brooklyn, New York – the site of its origin.

But Amy Varnadore of the landfill company said her firm probably would be able to unload only 2½ of the seven boxcars in Stuttgart by the deadline. Two employees unloaded the garbage and one drove a truck while three worked at the landfill itself, she said.

. "The inspecting (by PC&E) is slowing us down," she said, adding that rounding up qualified employees after a layoff took time.

Five of the boxcars were on the railroad siding April 28. That day, Rogers issued a restraining order blocking unloading of the boxcars until lawsuits regarding the disputed landfill are settled.

Two other boxcars arrived after April 28 and are on a separate spur in Stuttgart. Calling it a health hazard, Rogers or-

See GARBAGE, Page 15A

Garbage

● Continued from Page One
dered that those wastes be buried.

Attorney General Winston Bryant is trying to close the landfill, alleging that it doesn't comply with state regulations. The suit was combined with a similar one filed by Stuttgart-based Prosecuting Attorney Robert Dittrich.

Mobile home residents next to the spur complained about odors, prompting Bryant to file his suit. Rogers is expected to rule on the suit next week.

On Friday, odors could be detected 15 to 30 feet from the graffiti-laden boxcars, depending on how the wind was blowing. Odors could be smelled on occasion outside the closest mobile home, but not at the other mobile homes.

Helm said the unloading began at 8:25 a.m. when Dittrich removed a document referring to the restraining order from a boxcar door. Four loads – totaling about 30 tons of garbage – were transported to DeWitt and buried, he said.

None of the waste could be considered hazardous or infectious, Helm said.

"I have not noticed any different health-care items that I hand't already been noticing," he said. "I saw a few tires."

Helm said a "couple" of the boxcars continue to ooze an unknown liquid. PC&E has collected samples of the liquid for testing.

"We don't take responsibility for the cars sitting there 14 days and dripping," Varnadore responded.

Varnadore defended her firm's business, saying the New York garbage was safer than the DeWitt city garbage her landfill buries. The out-of-state waste constitutes about 75 percent of the landfill's business, she said.

She said the New York waste is highly compacted, contains no hazardous household wastes and has all recyclables already removed.

Varnadore led a reporter on a tour of the landfill, which is about a half-mile from her house. Waste brought to the landfill in the previous hour was nearly buried by the time of the tour. No odor could be detected.

Varnadore said the state has damaged the landfill company's relations with the New York recycler and other businesses, all in the name of politics. She said the landfill is being targeted because it is not municipally owned and does not have "deep pockets."

Despite the obstacles, Varnadore said she and her husband, Gray Varnadore, are not quitters.

"We're hell-bent on making a living," she said. "We have done our best."

Odoriferous odyssey

An Arkansas judge is to pen the final chapter this week on the odoriferous odyssey of seven boxcars on a siding at Stuttgart. They were full of ripening garbage from Brooklyn, N.Y., much of which may yet wander the rails back to the East Coast. The cars got there in late April, their foul cargo destined for a landfill at DeWitt. You can imagine the smell. Alas, folks living nearby didn't have to imagine. The stench sent them searching for clothespins. Let's hope none of the cars has to be sent back to Brooklyn, leaking all the way.

The judge in this case, Russell Rogers, has ordered the landfill operators to bury the wastes "with all due haste." It would be a blessed relief if he would do one more thing: Go ahead and order the landfill itself closed for failure to meet state standards. That might end the questionable practice of importing Yankee garbage.

In his ruling, Judge Rogers sliced through a haze of legal argumentation with Solomonic clarity: "The potential for harm from the garbage is greater sitting on a spur at Stuttgart or traveling several states on the railroad, oozing along the way, than burying it in even a non-complying landfill." Then he gave the landfill operators until noon today to empty the boxcars or ship the stuff back to Brooklyn.

However, the owners of the landfill — through an attorney — say their workforce disappeared during the course of this smelly controversy, and the deadline may go unmet. By Monday, a crew of six had been working since Friday, but only 2½ freight cars had been unloaded. As today's deadline approaches, several of the seven boxcars could be heading back East after all, polluting en route. If that happens, at least it may send a clear signal to other garbage merchants that the Natural State is out of bounds. Having issued an order to bury these remains or send them home, the judge can now see that it's obeyed. That would clear the air in more ways than one.

Garbage still in 4½ boxcars as deadline to unload passes

BY ANDY GOTLIEB
Democrat-Gazette State Desk

STUTTGART – A judge's deadline for the burial of New York garbage packed in seven railroad cars passed at noon Tuesday with four cars still loaded and a fifth still half-full.

Circuit-Chancery Judge Russell Rogers of Stuttgart ordered last week that the garbage be buried "with all due haste." The boxcars were to be unloaded and the contents taken to the SouthEast Arkansas Landfill near DeWitt (Arkansas County).

Whether the still-loaded boxcars will be returned to their origin, Star Recycling of Brooklyn, N.Y. – as Rogers ordered – or buried at the DeWitt landfill was not known Tuesday.

Rogers is expected to rule this week on a lawsuit filed by Attorney General Winston Bryant seeking to close the DeWitt landfill. Bryant has contended it doesn't comply with state regulations. His suit was combined with a similar one filed by Prosecuting Attorney Robert Dittrich of Stuttgart.

Rogers issued a restraining order April 28 blocking the unloading of boxcars until the lawsuit was settled. But last week, citing possible health hazards, he ordered the garbage buried.

A spokesman in Rogers' office said a ruling could be issued today.

Larry Wilson, a deputy director with the state Department of Pollution Control and Ecology, said the unloading seemed to go smoothly. Wilson oversees PC&E's Solid Waste Division.

"Our inspectors reported we saw no cause for alarm," he said. "They (landfill workers) ceased operations at noon as ordered."

Wilson said the contents of the waste stayed constant, with some non-infectious medical supplies included. A few of the cars continue to ooze an unknown liquid, he said.

Wilson said the odor produced by the garbage was remaining about the same. A PC&E inspector said Friday that odors could be detected 15 feet to 30 feet from the boxcars.

Amy Varnadore, a landfill spokesman, said her employees spread an odor control agent made from corncobs around the boxcars.

Varnadore said the unloaded boxcars will be returned to Star Recycling.

The restraining order made it difficult for the landfill to hold onto experienced workers to perform the unloading, Varnadore has said. She said the landfill's permit limits the amount of waste it can accept daily to about one boxcar load.

The Stuttgart Daily Leader, Thursday, May 21, 1992

Judge orders DeWitt landfill closed, Stuttgart operations halted

By KEITH F. TALLEY
Staff Writer

Circuit-Chancery Judge Russell Rogers of Stuttgart Wednesday ordered a DeWitt landfill to temporarily stop operations and closed a waste offloading facility near Stuttgart.

"It is therefore ordered that the defendants (Southeast Arkansas Landfill Inc.) are hereby temporarily restrained and enjoined from further operations of the landfill in Arkansas County for a period of 110 days... and that the offloading facility on the southern city limits of the city of Stuttgart shall be closed, all boxcars removed and the site cleaned up by Monday, June 1, 1992," Rogers wrote in yesterday's order.

The ruling was made because Attorney General Winston Bryant and Prosecuting Attorney Robert Dittrich of Stuttgart filed lawsuits in Arkansas County Chancery Court against the DeWitt landfill and the offloading facility.

Bryant filed a civil lawsuit April 23 against Southeast Arkansas Landfill Inc., the company that owns the landfill, for alleged violations of Arkansas laws regulating the storage, transportation and handling of solid wastes.

Dittrich filed a civil lawsuit April 28 against Gray Varnadore and the company responsible for the facility near Stuttgart because of the offending odor the offloading process created.

Varnadore is an owner of Southeast Arkansas Landfill Inc. and of Arkansas Waste Services Inc., the company operating the offloading site.

Rogers signed a temporary restraining order that prohibited the removal or storage of waste at the offloading facility when Dittrich filed his suit.

The controversy began when residents of a mobile home park located near the offloading site began complaining of an odor. The odor was coming from railroad boxcars sitting at the site.

The boxcars were full of trash that originated from Star Recycling Inc. out of Brooklyn, N.Y. The boxcars were being stored at the site before the offloaded trash was hauled to the DeWitt landfill.

"I am elated about the judge's

(See TRASH, page 2.)

ruling," Bryant said. "I think this indicates the state proved its case and presented substantial evidence that the DeWitt landfill should be shut down so that PC&E (Arkansas Department of Pollution Control and Ecology) can have time to determine whether or not the landfill operators are complying with the rules and regulations of the department (PC&E) and applicable state laws."

Bryant also said the ruling clearly indicates the remaining trash-laden boxcars are to be shipped back to New York.

On May 13 Rogers ordered eight boxcars of waste to be emptied and hauled to the DeWitt landfill before noon May 19. Only 2 1/2 boxcars had been unloaded when the deadline arrived. Five boxcars had been sitting at the offloading site and two boxcars were on a Southern Pacific railroad yard in Stuttgart when testimony concerning the lawsuits ended May 11.

"I'm pleased that Judge Rogers," Dittrich said, "saw our position concerning the unloading of waste within 75 feet of a residence (mobile home park)."

Both Bryant and Dittrich agreed the state presented substantial evidence that the landfill and offloading site posed a health hazard.

The defense argued during the hearing that other landfills in the area had worse problems than the DeWitt facility. The defense also questioned PC&E's contention that the landfill had a ground water problem.

"I still believe it's all politics," Varnadore said. "Rogers had absolutely no proof or any real documentation showing the landfill has any ground water problems.

"The high iron content in well 1 (ground water monitoring well) is probably what shut us down. Everyone knows the water in this part of the country runs high in iron.

"Judge Rogers showed a lack of intestinal fortitude in dealing with this matter," he added.

Varnadore said he was definitely going to appeal the ruling, but the boxcars would be returned to New York as soon as the railroad picks them up.

Arkansas Analytical, Inc.

501 North University
Little Rock, AR 72205

(501) 664-5661
FAX (501) 664-5891

May 21, 1992

Mr. Gray Varnadore
Southeast Arkansas Landfill, Inc.
Hwy 153
DeWitt, Arkansas 72042

Dear Mr. Varnadore,

Earlier this year we analyzed samples from your facility for a number of
parameters, including iron. Today an error was discovered in the value
originally reported for monitoring well number 7. The original value
reported was 550 mg/L (ppm). In reviewing the data at your request, it
was discovered that the actual value should have been 55 mg/L(ppm).
There was a decimal error in the original calculation.

Enclosed find a corrected copy of the original report with the value of
55 mg/L for iron in monitoring well number 7.

I apologize for the error. I would be happy to analyze another sample
from that well at no cost to your facility to provide updated
information on the iron content.

Sincerely,

Norma J. James

Norma J. James

"Hey, I just got a call from Judge Rogers. "Seems he would like for you to go ahead and off load the remaining four or five box cars at the rail spur before he rules on the case?"

I laughed. "You tell Judge Russell Rogers that I will wait on him to rule."

We both knew that Judge Rogers didn't want to have to send stinky rail cars loaded with garbage back across the country. Yet, I was not going to do anything until the Judge ruled on the case and allowed us to re-open. On May the 20th the ruling came to close the landfill temporarily. Clinton wouldn't have to answer Yankee Garbage questions during his campaign. Politics won again.

In late May I heard a knock at my door. The man introduced himself as a reporter, Richard Martin, from the Arkansas Times and said he would like to talk me.

"We smell a rat at the Times concerning this landfill issue. Did you know that Attorney General Winston Bryant was the key note speaker at the new Waste Management Landfill in Jefferson County?"

The article they printed was called, **Railroaded,** and part of it said: "Why is the state shutting down local landfills while big corporation operate dumps."

Wow, somebody was really watching what was going on and was willing to print it. It was great to have the truth printed about this issue, but way too late. My business was still closed and would be until the Presidential election was over.

My dad, wife, and I went to St. Louis to hear our appeal before the Eighth Circuit Court. We sat down and three Judges took their seats. My legal counsel, Charles Sydney Gibson, of Dermott, approached the podium. He opened his notes and started to read when Chief Justice Richard S. Arnold said, "Sit down counselor. This law is unconstitutional in the title as well as in content and I don't know what upsets me more. To know this law went through two bodies of government and signed by a governor with a degree in constitutional law. Or that it was passed over by two Federal Judges, who will be reprimanded for allowing this law suit to take up our time and come to this court."

The Judges asked the state legal counsel, Steve Weaver, a question. When Steve started to answer from a seated position at the counsel table, Justice Fagg, screamed.

"You get to the podium to address this court. He levitated out of that chair and I don't think his feet ever touched the ground between the counsel table and podium. Continue on pg. **102.**

The Stuttgart Daily Leader, Thursday, May 28, 1992

Lunch planned at landfill for city and state officials

PINE BLUFF – "Lunch at the landfill" will be held Friday for more than 200 city, county and state officeholders and others who will be attending the opening of the new Jefferson County Regional Landfill and Recycling Center north of Pine Bluff.

A project of Jefferson County and Waste Management of Arkansas, with assistance from the city of Pine Bluff, the official address opening the joint public/private venture will come from Attorney General Winston Bryant. Bryant has become one of the state's leading advocates for envi-

(See LANDFILL, page 2.)

Landfill

(Continued from page one.)

ronmental protection and for sound solid waste management practices.

"Through this partnership, an economically feasible, environmentally sound solution to solid waste management is in place for Southeast Arkansas," said Mickey Flood, regional vice president for Waste Management.

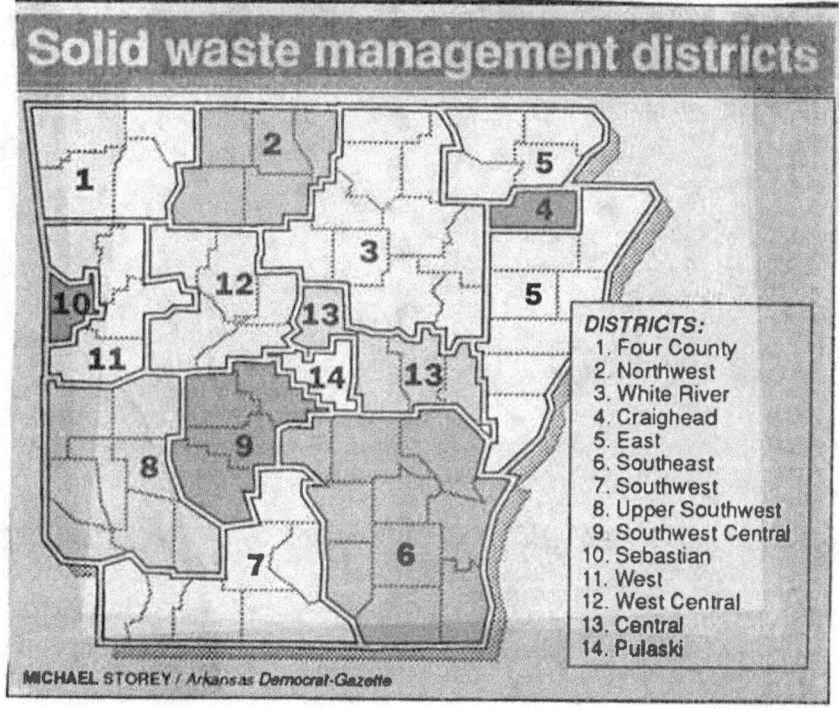

Solid waste management districts

DISTRICTS:
1. Four County
2. Northwest
3. White River
4. Craighead
5. East
6. Southeast
7. Southwest
8. Upper Southwest
9. Southwest Central
10. Sebastian
11. West
12. West Central
13. Central
14. Pulaski

MICHAEL STOREY / Arkansas Democrat-Gazette

RAIL ROADED

Why is the state shutting down a locally-owned landfill while big corporations operate dumps?

Gray Varnadore, with his son, can't understand why he can't bring in trash to fill his upgraded landfill at DeWitt.

BY RICHARD MARTIN

Winston Bryant was two for two on landfills this spring: He closed one down and opened another. The question is, did he close the right one?

The attorney general, who has appointed himself the state's environmental watchdog since taking office in 1990, was the featured speaker at the grand opening of the new Jefferson County Regional Landfill, north of Pine Bluff, on May 29. Even Bryant noted that there was some incongruity in holding such a ceremony for a waste dump:

"You may well be asking yourself why a public landfill even merits a grand opening," Bryant remarked in his speech to the assembled county judges, press, and municipal officials of southeast Arkansas. "It is because proper solid waste management is a critical concern, both locally and statewide, as well as a major concern throughout the country."

Indeed, the legislature declared a virtual state of emergency in 1991 for solid waste disposal and landfill capacity. And the new Jefferson County facility, an innovative partnership between local governments and multinational trash conglomerate Waste Management Inc. promises to solve southeast Arkansas's solid waste disposal needs for the foreseeable future.

Waste Management built the $3.2 million facility on land owned by the county, and will put another $250,000 an acre into developing and safeguarding the site as it fills. There's one problem: Waste Management of Arkansas, chosen by Jefferson County Judge Jack Jones for the project, has been assessed more than $350,000 in fines by the Department of Pollution Control and Ecology on two other landfills it operates in Pine Bluff and Little Rock—by far the heaviest fines assessed by the PC&E's solid waste division in the last decade.

Meanwhile, down the road at DeWitt, Gray Varnadore's Southeast Arkansas Landfill has been shut down, at least temporarily, by Bryant's one-man environmental crusade. The DeWitt landfill became a local *cause celebre* briefly in April when residents of a Stuttgart trailer park complained about the odor emanating from Varnadore's railroad off-loading facility, where refuse imported from New York was being shunted to trucks for the 30-mile trip to the landfill. In short order, Bryant and Arkansas County Prosecuting Attorney Robert Dittrich both filed lawsuits demanding that the garbage shipments be halted and the landfill itself shut down.

"Boxcars Ooze Waste," the headlines said. Newly minted environmentalists statewide were outraged at the idea of the Natural State becoming a dumping ground for Yankee garbage. And Circuit-Chancery Judge Russell Rogers, after hearing testimony from PC&E officials that the landfill was not in compliance with state regulations and had violated its permit by expanding its service area, issued a ruling closing the landfill for 110 days and halting the out-of-state shipments.

The public outcry, portraying an operator dumping out-of-state trash in a substandard facility, was once again not quite in accordance with the facts. While the Varnadore landfill has been in and out of trouble with PC&E and with creditors for years—"a nuisance since the day it was permitted" in 1982 is how one state geologist describes it—an inspection by PC&E inspector Keith Helms on April 13 found no "problem indicators" and no violations in construction or waste handling at the facility. And the groundwater analysis on the site in January, which initially indicated high levels of iron, was discovered to be in error in May—after Judge Rogers had closed down the facility.

"The PC&E, who know well that 80 percent of the landfills in this state are substandard, has been dragged into this by the attorney general," protests Charles Sidney Gibson of Dermott, Varnadore's attorney. "Mr. Bryant is simply pandering to public opinion."

In fact, groundwater tests at two Waste Management facilities—Brushy Island, in North Little Rock, and Shannon Road, in Pine Bluff—have revealed levels of metals and dissolved solids that dwarf those at the Southeast Arkansas Landfill (an October, 1991 test at Shannon Road, for example, found 4880 milligrams per liter of dissolved solids in one well—compared to a high of 841 milligrams per liter at DeWitt).

"Despite the biased interpretation of data by the company," notes an internal PC&E memo on the Shannon Road landfill written by geologist Tony Morris and dated February 19, 1991, "the shallow groundwater contains some of the highest sulfate, chloride, [and] total dissolved solids values in Arkansas." The memo goes on to recommend that "Landowners within one-half mile of the site should be notified of the potential health hazards associated with using the shallow groundwater."

As for the Yankee garbage, Gray Varnadore is hardly the only landfill operator importing trash into Arkansas: at least six other facilities currently accept out-of-state waste, according to PC&E records—including a Western Waste facility at Texarkana which faces stiff penalties itself and may soon be socked with the heaviest fine in Arkansas landfill history, according to PC&E sources.

"If we could get in-state garbage, we wouldn't be bringing it in," protests Varnadore, who claims he has been unfairly targeted as a polluter. "But we're trying to compete with the largest waste disposal company in the world, and if we can't compete in the district, we're forced to bring it in from out of state."

Therein lies the core of the landfill dilemma, for Varnadore as well as for other small towns and waste-disposal firms around the state.

Legislation passed in 1991 established 12 regional Solid Waste Management Districts, placed restrictions on disposal of waste from outside each district, and called for the development of adequate, safe landfills through regional planning and funding, and through such private-public partnerships as the Jefferson County facility. One result, as giants such as Waste Management take over the large regional contracts, is that smaller operations like the DeWitt landfill will be squeezed out. In fact, plans developed by the 10-county Southeast Arkansas Regional Waste District propose six scenarios for the future—none of which include the Varnadore landfill.

Arkansas has a severe shortage of landfill capacity in the northwest part of the state, with its hilly, porous topography, and a surplus of

(From left) Waste Management executive Mickey Flood, Attorney General Winston Bryant, and Jefferson County Judge Jack Jones look over the new landfill that promises southeast Arkansas's trash needs.

capacity in the southeastern flatlands. While the new regional system allows for interdistrict transfers in emergency situations, it could hamper the development of a system that would bury the garbage where it belongs. What's more, the U.S. Supreme Court ruled recently that state bans on the importation of out-of-state waste are illegal barriers to interstate commerce—meaning that Gray Varnadore has a constitutional right to bring in waste from any state in the Union.

The development of a regional system to replace the unplanned quilt of 138 landfills around the state is probably the only way to dig our way out of the trash mess, and since building landfills is an expensive proposition, it may be that only big corporations like Waste Management will survive. (The largest waste disposal company in the U.S., operating in 48 states and 20 countries, Waste Management is spending some $240 million on an Arizona landfill that is projected to generate billions of dollars in profits over the next half-century). PC&E officials privately acknowledge—and deputy director Larry Wilson claimed on the stand in a hearing on the DeWitt landfill—that working with a large company is preferable to dealing with an individual landfill because Waste Management can afford to build state-of-the-art facilities, not to mention pay stiff fines when their landfills fail. And Waste Management is not necessarily an unprogressive company: it has based its corporate strategy around a "Recycle America" program which takes the long view toward solving waste disposal problems, and the two dirty landfills for which it has been penalized were acquired, not constructed by the company. The Jefferson County landfill is touted as having the potential to be one of the safest in the state and will eventually include, according to the company, a recycling center, compost dump, and a used tire recycling facility. It's a safe bet that the future of solid waste will look something like this.

None of which helps Varnadore, whose father started in the trash business 10 years ago and who along with an investor has plowed $350,000 into the 80-acre landfill site near his home outside DeWitt. At press time Varnadore was appealing Rogers' ruling and attempting to find another rail spur where he can bring in the trash he needs to keep the operation going.

"They've said there's an emergency situation with landfills in this state, that landfill capacity is a valuable resource—but they've shut us down," Varnadore complains. "It's a disgrace to this state that I have to go to Brooklyn to find waste—especially when Waste Management has been running an open dump up there [at Shannon Road] for years."

The Stuttgart Daily Leader, Friday, June 26, 1992–

PC&E official defends closed DeWitt landfill

LITTLE ROCK (AP) — A geologist for the state pollution control agency says tests show that a landfill closed by a judge last month could have a future.

A memo from the state Pollution Control and Ecology Commission says water samples taken at South-East Arkansas Landfill — also known as SEAL — at DeWitt showed the groundwater wasn't seriously contaminated.

Tony Morris, a geologist in PC&E's Solid Waste Division, said the landfill's future is muddy.

"Our next step is to decide what these numbers mean and form a plan of attack for the landfill," he said. The operations at the facility need upgrading, he said. "As far as sites go, in my opinion, it's not a bad site."

Samples taken by PC&E on June 3-4 show no manmade substances known as volatile organics were found in any of the seven wells tested at SEAL. A June 15 memo from PC&E said that levels of several elements tested declined from those found in previous tests of water at the landfill.

Results of past testing were used as evidence in hearings to close the landfill. Circuit-Chancery Russell Rogers of Stuttgart on May 19 agreed to close the dump for 119 days to allow the state to conduct tests and take other action that "it deems proper administratively."

Rogers ruled in a suit brought by Attorney General Winston Bryant, who sought an order revoking SEAL's permit from PC&E.

"We knew the water was going to come back this way even before they took the samples," said Amy Varnadore, a landfill co-owner.

(See LANDFILL, page 9.)

Landfill

(Continued from page one.)

Bryant had argued in his suit, filed in April, that the landfill hadn't complied with state standards.

He took his action after residents at a mobile home park near a Stuttgart railroad spur complained about odors from garbage-filled boxcars. The garbage in the boxcars, from New York, was destined for the landfill.

"Some things he's (Bryant) done are good, but his main concern is seeing how good it will look in the newspaper," said attorney Charles Sidney Gibson of Dermott, who represents the landfill operators.

But Bryant has said politics played no role in his decision to file the suit. He did not immediately return a telephone call to his office Thursday.

In seeking revocation of the landfill's permit, Bryant cited permit violations, the landfill owners' poor financial status and improvements needed at the landfill site.

—DeWitt, Arkansas, Era-Enterprise, Thursday, July 2, 1992

Water Samples Within Acceptable Ranges At SouthEast Ark. Landfill

Water samples from the Arkansas County landfill that Attorney General Winston Bryant successfully sued to close last month are "within acceptable ranges," according to a state agency.

Samples taken by the state Department of Pollution Control and Ecology on June 3-4 show that no volatile organics — man-made compounds such as degreasing agents — were found in any of the seven wells tested at the SouthEast Arkansas Landfill.

A PC&E memo dated June 15 says that the levels of several elements tested in the water declined from those found in previous tests. Past test results were used as evidence in hearings to close the landfill.

The attorney for the DeWitt landfill owners said Wednesday the results vindicate their contentions about the way they have been treated by Bryant.

"Some things he's done are good, but his main concern is seeing how good it will look in the newspaper," said Charles Sidney Gibson of Dermott (Chicot County).

"We knew the water was going to come back this way even before they took the samples," said Amy Varnadore, a landfill co-owner.

Bryant filed a lawsuit in April contending that the landfill doesn't comply with state standards. Residents of a mobile home by a Stuttgart railroad spur complained about odors, prompting Bryant to file the suit. The landfill company had been using the spur to unload boxcars filled with garbage from New York.

On May 19, Circuit-Chancery Judge Russell Rogers of Stuttgart sided with Bryant, prohibiting the landfill from operating for 110 days while the state conducted tests and took "whatever action it deems proper administratively."

Since then, Bryant has asked PC&E to revoke SouthEast's permit. He cited permit violations, the landfill owners' poor financial status and improvements needed at the landfill site.

Tony Morris, a geologist in PC&E's Solid Waste Division, said he didn't know what kind of future the landfill faces.

"Our next step is to decide what these numbers mean and form a plan of attack for the landfill," he said, adding that the operation needs upgrading. "As far as sites go, in my opinion, it's not a bad site."

Water samples from landfill pass state test

BY ANDY GOTLIEB
Democrat-Gazette State Desk

Water samples from the Arkansas County landfill that Attorney General Winston Bryant successfully sued to close last month are "within acceptable ranges," according to a state agency.

Samples taken by the state Department of Pollution Control and Ecology on June 3-4 show that no volatile organics — man-made compounds such as degreasing agents — were found in any of the seven wells tested at the SouthEast Arkansas Landfill.

A PC&E memo dated June 15 says that the levels of several elements tested in the water declined from those found in previous tests. Past test results were used as evidence in hearings to close the landfill.

The attorney for the DeWitt landfill owners said Wednes-

See LANDFILL, Page 8B

Landfill

• Continued from Arkansas Page

day the results vindicate their contentions about the way they have been treated by Bryant.

"Some things he's done are good, but his main concern is seeing how good it will look in the newspaper," said Charles Sidney Gibson of Dermott (Chicot County).

"We knew the water was going to come back this way even before they took the samples," said Amy Varnadore, a landfill co-owner.

Bryant, who was at Crater of Diamonds State Park in Murfreesboro (Pike County) on Wednesday, was unavailable for comment, a spokesman said. Bryant has previously denied he was politically motivated to close the SouthEast landfill.

Bryant filed a lawsuit in April contending that the landfill doesn't comply with state standards. Residents of a mobile home by a Stuttgart railroad spur complained about odors, prompting Bryant to file the suit. The landfill company had been using the spur to unload boxcars filled with garbage from New York.

On May 19, Circuit-Chancery Judge Russell Rogers of Stuttgart sided with Bryant, prohibiting the landfill from operating for 110 days while the state conducted tests and took "whatever action it deems proper administratively."

Since then, Bryant has asked PC&E to revoke SouthEast's permit. He cited permit violations, the landfill owners' poor financial status and improvements needed at the landfill site.

Tony Morris, a geologist in PC&E's Solid Waste Division, said he didn't know what kind of future the landfill faces.

"Our next step is to decide what these numbers mean and form a plan of attack for the landfill," he said, adding that the operation needs upgrading. "As far as sites go, in my opinion, it's not a bad site."

Owners trying to reopen landfill

But waste district isn't interested in offers by troubled site

BY ANDY GOTLIEB
Democrat-Gazette State Desk

Three months after a judge closed their operation, owners of a controversial landfill near DeWitt continue their quest to reopen the landfill in one form or another.

But two proposals made to the Southeast Arkansas Regional Waste District — which is developing a waste-disposal plan for a 10-county area —have been met with a lukewarm response.

And a proposed consent order by the state Department of Pollution Control and Ecology calls for repairs and improvements that would cost $80,000 to $85,000, according to Gray Varnadore, one of the owners of the SouthEast Arkansas Landfill (SEAL), six miles east of DeWitt (Arkansas County).

Varnadore said he doubted the landfill would be allowed to reopen if those improvements were made.

"It's not a matter of affording it," he said. "It's a matter of whether that's enough. They keep throwing obstacles in our way. It's still a political move to keep this landfill shut down."

PC&E spokesman Becky Allison said details of the proposed consent order cannot be released until Varnadore decides whether to sign the order. She said PC&E is awaiting a response.

The landfill got a spate of unwelcome publicity in April when Attorney General Winston Bryant filed a lawsuit contending that the landfill failed to meet state standards.

Residents near a Stuttgart railroad spur that SEAL used for unloading trash had complained about odors, prompting Bryant's suit. The garbage unloaded at the spur originated from a Brooklyn, N.Y., recycling firm.

On May 19, Circuit-Chancery Judge Russell Rogers of Stuttgart ordered the landfill closed for 110 days while the state conducted tests and took any necessary administrative actions.

In July, Varnadore offered to sell the landfill to the waste district for $1. In return, the district would have paid a royalty of $2 per cubic yard of garbage deposited at SEAL. The company is requiring a minimum of 600 yards be delivered a day, five days a week, under that system.

In a new offer advanced last week, Varnadore said he would sell the 200-acre landfill to the waste district for $2.88 million. Also, a hauling subsidiary of SEAL would be paid $18.65 per ton to pick up, transport and bury the garbage. SEAL's minimum demands are about 880 tons of trash a week under the new offer.

"To be real honest with you, they didn't seem real interested in it," Varnadore said.

Warren (Bradley County) Mayor Gregg Reep, chairman of the waste district, said Varnadore's landfill has two problems: its difficulties with the

See LANDFILL, Page 3B

Landfill

• Continued from Arkansas Page

state and its location.

"We're having trouble seeing how we can gain very much going that far," Reep said, noting that the landfill is in the extreme northeast corner of the district.

Although no decisions have been made, Reep said many waste district members want to keep numerous alternatives open at all times.

"If we lock ourselves into some kind of deal like the Varnadores', we pull the options out from under us," he said.

Varnadores Offer Landfill Site To Southeast Ark. Waste Dist.

Owners of the SouthEast Arkansas Landfill Inc. (SEAL) have offered a proposal to the Southeast Arkansas Waste District.

Gray and Amy Varnadore, owners of SEAL propose to convey their landfill to the Southeast Arkansas Waste District for the sum of $1.00 and the promise of the District to pay a royalty of $2.00 per cubic yard deposited into the landfill with a quantity of 60 yards a day guaranteed five days a week.

According to the proposal the SEAL facility is sited in an excellent alluvial clay formation six miles east of DeWitt. The facility has 200 permitted acres, eighty of which has been engineered for a high volume operation. The remaining 80 acre capacity is 1,463,007-2,883,007 cubic yards. The additional 120 acres would guarantee the district a use-life of seventy years.

"It's not a desperation move," said attorney Charles Sidney Gibson of Dermott, who represents landfill owners, Mr. and Mrs. Varnadore.

"It's a business proposal. It's an alternate proposal for the Varnadores to market their landfill and not take out-of-state waste."

Gibson contended that the Varnadores' landfill could be operated at far lower costs than other sites elsewhere in the district. He said development costs at the DeWitt landfill are $150,000 per acre, compared with $250,000 per acre for the new Jefferson County landfill.

"Those costs have to be absorbed in tipping fees," he said, referring to the price charged to dump garbage.

Warren (Bradley County) Mayor Greg Reep, the waste district's chairman, said the Varnadore's proposal has been placed on the district's agenda. He said he knew little about it.

"We're just going to have to listen to what they say," Reep said. "I'm sure it will be taken into consideration along with the plan developed by The Mehlburger Firm."

The Little Rock engineering firm is finishing work on a waste disposal plan for the district's future needs as required by state law, Reep said.

Reep did not immediately rule out the Varnadores' plan.

"Depending upon what kind of deal they offer, there may be some savings," he said. "The biggest problem in the southern part of the southeast district is that they're a long way off."

But Gibson said the DeWitt landfill —

(Continued on page 8)

92

Varnadores Offer

(Continued from page 1)

located in the district's northeast corner — is about the same distance away from southern counties as the Jefferson County landfill in the district's north-central portion.

The waste district is made up of 10 counties including Arkansas. Arkansas County Judge Bobby Ashcraft and mayor of DeWitt, Carroll Lester, serve on the committee. Mayor Lester attends the meetings and keeps the DeWitt City Council informed as to any district actions.

Varnadore's porposal is being considered along with several others, said Mayor Reep, the district chairman.

Like, the state's other solid waste districts, the southeast district is struggling to come up with a state-mandated solid waste disposal plan, Reep said. The district has hired a Little Rock engineering firm to work on a plan for the region.

A seemingly popular option is to have two landfills meeting state and federal regulation in the district. The northern end would use the new public-private landfill in Jefferson County. Building a new landfill for the southern counties appears to be under strong consideration.

Keith Bauder of The Mehlburger Firm Inc. said the Varnadore landfill has the problem of poor location. The landfill is in the district's northeast corner.

"It's on the wrong side of the district for the southern people," Bauder said, indicating that his firm will consider other options. "This plan is not the Ten Commandments."

"We don't gain on transportation costs," Reep said. "We still have to check the bottomline costs."

Jefferson County Judge Jack Jones contended that the new landfill in Jefferson County already offers cheaper

dumped in Jefferson County and city garbage is hauled by city trucks to Phillips County.

According to PC&E the local landfill site is one of the better sites in the state and possibly has a future.

According to a ground water sampling at SEAL June 3 and 4 the water chemistry from the well system is within acceptable ranges. "It should be noted that several parameters declined considerably over past data submitted by the company. This difference could be attributed to inadequate purging prior to sampling or some other sampling problems," the report stated.

Anyone interested in the site of the District Waste Landfill should contact Judge Ashcraft or Mayor Lester and express your feelings.

Varnadore outlined a scenario where transportation costs to his facility would dwarf construction costs for a new landfill. "Your landfill is certainly in the running," Monticello Mayor Harold West said. "We're not locked into anything."

Mr. Varnadore stated that a district waste facility would improve the local economy, provide more jobs, and save the city and county monies in transportation cost.

Reep said later that Jones was referring to the "host fee" the county charges. When combined with the dumping fee, the rates at the Jefferson County facility are significantly higher, he said.

Besides Reep, several members expressed concerns about added transportation costs that would result from the location of Varnadore's landfill. However, Hamburg (Ashley County) Mayor Boyce Harrod said those costs are becoming less important considering the shortage of landfill space.

"We'll see the day, even in our lifetime, when it will be economically feasible to transport waste 100 miles," he said.

Arkansas Democrat 🦅 Gazette
● ● THURSDAY SEPTEMBER 10, 1992

Despite expiration of court order, landfill at DeWitt remains closed

BY ANDY GOTLIEB
Democrat-Gazette State Desk

Chances are remote that a controversial landfill near De-Witt will reopen any time soon, even though a court-ordered 110-day closure has ended, landfill owner Gray Varnadore said Wednesday.

Two usage proposals for the SouthEast Arkansas Landfill (SEAL) to the Southeast Arkansas Regional Waste District apparently will be rejected by the district, Warren (Bradley County) Mayor Gregg Reep said.

"I don't think there's a whole lot of interest in pursuing their plans," Reep, who chairs the 10-county waste district, said. "There's a lot of things that concern a lot of our members."

Varnadore said he has not agreed to a proposed consent order by the state Department of Pollution Control and Ecology calling for $80,000 to $85,000 in repairs before reopening. Before dealing with the consent order, he plans to appeal the court decision that led to the landfill being closed. He said he is waiting for a transcript of the hearing.

"Until we can get use of the railroad spur, there's no enough local volume for us t reopen," Varnadore said.

Varnadore's landfill, i Arkansas County six miles eas of DeWitt, drew publicity i April when Attorney Genera Winston Bryant filed a lawsu contending that the landfil failed to meet state standards.

Mobile home residents near Stuttgart railroad spur SEA used for unloading prompte the suit by complaining abou odors. The garbage unloaded a the spur originated from Brooklyn, N.Y., recycling firm

See LANDFILL, Page 3

Landfill

● Continued from Page 1B

On May 19, Circuit-Chancery Judge Russell Rogers of Stuttgart ordered the landfill closed for 110 days while the state conducted tests and took administrative actions.

After completing tests that showed water samples from the landfill within acceptable contamination limits and proposing the consent order, PC&E has had little contact with SEAL, department spokesman Becky Allison said.

Reep cited three reasons why the waste district is opposed to Varnadore's offers.

The landfill's inconvenient location in the extreme northeast part of the district, environmental concerns and the long-term contracts Varnadore desires are the main drawbacks, Reep said.

Under one offer, Varnadore would sell the landfill for $1 in exchange for royalties on garbage deposited at the facility. A second offer featured the sale of the landfill for $2.88 million along with a per-ton fee for pickup and disposal.

The waste district appears likely to endorse a plan calling for two landfills within the district: An as-yet unspecified facility for the southern counties and the new public-private landfill in Jefferson County for the northern counties, Reep said.

Should Varnadore regain the right to use the Stuttgart spur, economics may push him toward contracting for out-of-state waste, he said.

"That's not what we want to do, but if we're forced to we'll look for it," he said.

94

Arkansas Democrat ✠ Gazette

● ● SATURDAY, OCTOBER 3, 1992

Out-of-state waste may be heading in

BY DOUG THOMPSON
Democrat-Gazette Benton Bureau

The state Department of Pollution Control and Ecology probably will lose a lawsuit over keeping out-of-state garbage from Arkansas landfills, deputy director Larry Wilson said Friday.

Given the rising cost of landfills under new federal regulations, many of the state's 14 regional solid waste management districts probably will seek out-of-state garbage to help pay the bills, he said.

The districts will retain control over issuing new permits for landfills, Wilson said.

The state won its fight to keep non-Arkansas garbage out at the lower court level. But "there's been a couple of Supreme Court cases since then" that ruled against laws blocking interstate waste transportation, he said.

"From what the judges said on the bench in our appeal and what our lawyers tell us, it's not real encouraging," Wilson said.

The suit is on appeal to the 8th U.S. Circuit Court of Appeals. It stems from a federal bankruptcy court ruling. Landfill operator D. Gray Varnadore of DeWitt protested provisions of state Act 870 of 1989 and Act 319 of 1991 that prohibit out-of-state customers, shutting down his landfill operation in DeWitt.

"They knew it was unconstitutional when they passed it," Varnadore said Friday. "They only did it to delay importation of out-of-state waste, to make us go through the legal system for three years."

Varnadore protested the restrictions under U.S. constitutional provisions that prohibit restriction of interstate commerce. The case was argued before the appeals court last month, Varnadore said.

He said a ruling could be weeks away. Act 870 prohibits a waste management district from accepting any trash from across district lines, which included out-of-state trash. Act 319 al-

lowed a district to bring in up to 50 tons of trash a day from the outside.

The 14 districts are responsible for planning waste disposal in their areas. The districts vary in size from one county to 11 and in population from 349,660 to 68,956.

State law allows counties with more than 50,000 people to form one-county districts. But districts that small may not be financially viable under stringent new federal landfill standards, Wilson said. Asked if the 50,000 population limit was too low, Wilson said, "We have our doubts about it."

See DUMP, Page 4B

Dump

● Continued from Page 1B

For example, developing a 108-acre landfill in Benton under almost ideal geological conditions will cost about $1.5 million, he said.

And the Four County Waste

'If the tipping fees are already over $100 in some places, they can afford to ship a long way to a place where the tipping fees are cheaper.'

Management District in Northwest Arkansas is located in a geological region "where we've had trouble with every landfill," Wilson said.

Getting a landfill that meets federal requirements will be expensive, he said.

Landfill costs, or "tipping fees," make up about 20 percent of the average waste disposal bill of an Arkansas resident. But it is a major expense for cities and counties, one that could triple under the stringent federal rules going into effect in October 1993, according to federal Environmental Protection Agency projections.

"The average rate nationwide is $30 a ton.

Some parts of the country have rates of $100 a ton and more.

In Arkansas, it's about $12 to $13 a ton," Wilson said.

There will not be a sudden rise in costs because districts have had time to prepare, Wilson said. And costs won't rise as rapidly in some districts, he said. But the trend is definitely upward.

Those rising expenses, both in Arkansas and out of it, will provide incentives to districts to seek out-of-state customers, he said.

"If the tipping fees are already over $100 in some places, they can afford to ship a long way to a place where the tipping fees are cheaper," Wilson said.

"If a district in Arkansas is facing landfill expense, it's going to look for outside customers."

8th Circuit rules state can't ban imported garbage

BY ANDY GOTLIEB
Democrat-Gazette State Desk

A state cannot ban landfill operators from bringing in out-of-state garbage because that prohibition violates the commerce clause of the U.S. Constitution, the 8th U.S. Circuit Court of Appeals at St. Louis said in reversing a decision.

The ruling Friday is a victory for the SouthEast Arkansas Landfill near DeWitt (Arkansas County), which sued in response to so-called "Yankee trash" laws passed in Arkansas in 1989 and 1991. The laws, which created solid waste districts, banned new landfills from taking in garbage from outside the districts and severely restricted how much out-of-district waste could be received by existing landfills.

The lawsuit was dismissed in U.S. District Court. Friday's opinion, written by Chief Judge Richard Arnold, ordered the lower court to issue a new ruling that took into consideration the 8th Circuit's findings.

"We hold that portions of the acts in question discriminate on their face against solid waste originating outside the state of Arkansas," Arnold wrote.

"It took four years for the judicial system to work for us, but Judge Arnold and the 8th Circuit weren't influenced by the petty politics going on in Arkansas," Gray Varnadore, one of SEAL's owners, said.

The original lawsuit was filed against the Department of Pollution Control and Ecology in April 1990. At the time, Varnadore was seeking to accept 6,000 cubic yards of sewage sludge a day from Baltimore. PC&E received a temporary restraining order against SEAL to review the landfill's plans.

Varnadore said he would probably seek approval from the PC&E to reopen his landfill. In the absence of locally generated wastes, he said, he would be forced to take out-of-state trash.

During the fall, Varnadore made two proposals to the Southeast Arkansas Regional Waste District, of which Arkansas County is a part, about using his landfill. The proposals met with little interest.

Steve Weaver, PC&E's chief legal counsel, said the decision shouldn't mean much for the state.

"This does not mean the state will become the dumping ground for the nation," Weaver said. He indicated that because the ruling applies to all states, there is no particular advantage in sending trash to Arkansas.

Varnadore's attorney, Charles Sidney Gibson of Dermott (Chicot County), agreed with Weaver that Arkansas wouldn't become a dumping ground for out-of-state waste. Most landfills won't find it economically feasible, he said.

The ruling could actually improve the environmental soundness of some Arkansas landfills, Gibson said. Because of the higher volume operators like Varnadore can expect, they will be able to better afford the improvements now being required, he said.

In the 12-page ruling, Arnold cited a ruling issued by the U.S. Supreme Court earlier this year that pertained to a similar situation in Michigan.

"Unless there is something showing that the out-of-state waste excluded is more than harmful than the in-state waste allowed, the statute must fail," he wrote.

The U.S. Supreme Court ruling came nine days after Weaver

See GARBAGE, Page 10B

Garbage

● Continued from Page 1B

made his arguments before the appeals court.

"After that, the 8th Circuit position was kind of expected," he said, noting that he would keep open a possible appeal to the high court.

Varnadore's landfill drew publicity in June when Attorney General Winston Bryant filed a lawsuit contending that the facility did not meet state standards.

Mobile home residents near a Stuttgart railroad spur SEAL used for unloading complained about odors to Bryant, prompting the suit.

The garbage unloaded at the spur originated from a Brooklyn, N.Y., recycling firm.

On May 19, Circuit-Chancery Judge Russell Rogers of Stuttgart ordered the landfill closed for 110 days while the state conducted tests.

He also prohibited the landfill from using the Stuttgart spur.

The landfill remains closed, even though PC&E tests showed water samples from the facility within acceptable contamination limits.

PC&E has told SEAL it needs $80,000 to $85,000 in improvements before it can reopen.

United States Court of Appeals

FOR THE EIGHTH CIRCUIT

No. 92-1386EA

In re Southeast Arkansas
Landfill, Inc.,

      Debtor.

Southeast Arkansas Landfill,
Inc.,

      Appellant,

v.

State of Arkansas, Department
of Pollution Control and
Ecology,

      Appellee.

On Appeal from the United
States District Court
for the Eastern District
of Arkansas.

Submitted: September 18, 1992

Filed: December 11, 1992

Before RICHARD S. ARNOLD, Chief Judge, FAGG and MAGILL, Circuit
Judges.

RICHARD S. ARNOLD, Chief Judge.

The question presented is the validity under the Commerce
Clause of two Acts of the Arkansas General Assembly regulating the
disposal of solid waste, Act 870 of 1989 and Act 319 of 1991.
Southeast Arkansas Landfill, Inc., a debtor in bankruptcy, brought
this case as an adversary proceeding against the Arkansas

Department of Pollution Control and Ecology (PC&E), the State agency charged with the administration of these statutes. The District Court referred the matter to a bankruptcy judge for recommended findings and conclusions, see 28 U.S.C. § 157(b), (c). The Bankruptcy Judge recommended that the Acts be upheld, and that the debtor's suit for an injunction against their enforcement be dismissed. The District Court accepted this recommendation and entered judgment accordingly. This appeal followed.

We hold that portions of the Acts in question discriminate on their face against solid waste originating outside the State of Arkansas. State statutes having this effect violate the Commerce Clause unless the State proves that out-of-state waste is for some reason more harmful than in-state waste. City of Philadelphia v. New Jersey, 437 U.S. 617, 629 (1978). The State has not come forward with any such proof, and, indeed, does not suggest that it could do so. Accordingly, we hold that the statutes in question, to the extent indicated in this opinion, are unconstitutional, and we reverse the judgment of the District Court.

I.

Act 870 of 1989 was approved on March 22 of that year. It establishes a planning and management process for solid waste. The hallmark of this process is that it is to proceed on a regional basis. The statute divides the State into eight regions, referred to as Regional Solid Waste Planning Districts, each to be managed, within certain limits, by a Regional Solid Waste Planning Board. The principal portion of the Act which gives rise to the present controversy is Section 6. This Section reads as follows:

> SECTION 6. Until January 31, 1991, no existing landfill shall expand its service area outside of the District in which it is located. Existing landfills that currently serve areas outside of their respective

> Districts shall not increase the total amount
> of solid waste originating from outside their
> Districts by more than twenty percent (20%) of
> the total solid waste received at such
> facility. No new landfill shall be allowed to
> receive solid waste outside the boundaries of
> the District in which it is located until
> after January 31, 1991. No new applications
> for landfill permits seeking to dispose of
> solid waste originating outside of the
> district created hereunder, or that propose to
> dispose of solid waste originating from
> outside such district, shall be accepted or
> processed by the Commission or a regional
> solid waste planning board, unless such
> applications were pending before the
> Department of Pollution Control and Ecology as
> of March 1, 1989. All landfill permit
> applications shall specify the service areas
> which the landfill will serve under the
> permit.

Thus, under Act 870 as originally passed, landfills are, as a general rule, forbidden to accept waste from outside the boundaries of the Regional Solid Waste Planning District in which they are located. There are some exceptions to this ban. Landfills already serving areas outside of their districts may continue to do so, but the total amount of waste originating from outside the district may not increase by more than 20% of the total solid waste received at the landfill. No new applications for landfill permits seeking to dispose of out-of-district waste are to be processed, unless they were already pending before PC&E on March 1, 1989. However, under the original Section 6, after January 31, 1991, existing landfills could expand their service area outside of the districts in which they are located, and new landfills could begin to receive out-of-district waste.

As the January 31, 1991, date in Section 6 of Act 870 demonstrates, the statute was, in part, a moratorium, not an absolute prohibition. The next regular session of the General Assembly convened in January of 1991. As the end of the month drew near, it became apparent that a comprehensive new statute, amending Act 870, would not be ready by the January 31 deadline. Accordingly, on January 31, 1991, a new statute, Act 9 of 1991, became law. The new statute repeated all of the substantive provisions of Section 6 of Act 870, but substituted a new deadline: March 2, 1991.

The judgment of the District Court, dismissing the debtor's complaint in this adversary proceeding, is reversed, and this cause is remanded to that Court with directions to fashion equitable relief consistent with the principles laid down in this opinion. It is not our intention to invalidate or interfere with any provisions of Act 870 of 1989 or Act 319 of 1991 that do not discriminate against interstate commerce, and we note that both statutes contain severability clauses. Act 870, Section 13; Act 319, Section 7. In addition, nothing in this opinion in any way

diminishes the right of the State to require landfills within its borders to meet health and safety standards.

Reversed and remanded with instructions.

A true copy.

Attest:

CLERK, U. S. COURT OF APPEALS, EIGHTH CIRCUIT.

They lit into Steve about even being there. They told Weaver the state passed this law to put this man (me and my family) out of business. We were told to leave. It didn't last 10 minutes and we were on our way out the door.

That was awesome. Finally, Judge's with balls. Too bad Governor Clinton and the state legislators weren't here to get this ass chewing instead of Weaver. They are the ones that deserve it. However, it was bullshit we had to go all the way to the Eight Circuit-Court to find a Judge that would call this law what it was, unconstitutional and an illegal action to close my business

So we won! Now what does that mean for the landfill?

*****

We won the legal battle but we were now broke and didn't have the money to get the landfill back into operation. I offered the entire business to our Solid Waste District, for one dollar, plus a lifetime royalty. They hired Genesis Environmental (a top Environmental company in Arkansas) to do a study to determine the quality of the site and feasibility of using it. At the District Solid Waste meeting Genesis Environmental give their recommendation that the District should buy the facility.

Arkansas County Judge, Sonny Cox, jumped up and said he'd sue the district, if the district bought the landfill. Jefferson County Judge, Jack Jones, made the motion to vote to not vote on the issue and let it die. And that is just how the Board voted. To vote to not vote.

The decision was made in 1992 and was the last straw for our business. I ended up selling the landfill in 1999 to a waste company in northeastern Arkansas. Eaton Moery Services, operated the facility from 2001 until August 31, 2012, when they filed for chapter 7 bankruptcy.

In the end we were exonerated however, we were never compensated for our losses. The only ones that received compensation were the damn lawyers. Because of liars and lawyers and politicians, we lost not only our business, but also lost the farm.

The End